# An Ear to the Ground

# An Ear to the Ground

## An Anthology of Contemporary American Poetry

Edited by

*Marie Harris and Kathleen Aguero*

*The University of Georgia Press*
Athens and London

The editors would like to extend their warm thanks
to the Merck Family Fund; Pam Palmquist; R#1;
Karen Orchard; the essayists, poets, and friends who
sparked our choices and pointed us in new directions; and,
again, to Charter Weeks and Richard Hoffman.

Designed by Kathi L. Dailey
Set in Mergenthaler Electra with Olive Antique
Typeset by G&S Typesetters
Printed and bound by Thomson-Shore
The paper in this book meets the guidelines for
permanence and durability of the Committee on
Production Guidelines for Book Longevity of the
Council on Library Resources.

Printed in the United States of America

93  92  91  90  89      5  4  3  2  1

Library of Congress Cataloging in Publication Data

An Ear to the ground.

    Bibliography: p.
    1. American poetry—20th century.   I. Harris, Marie.
II. Aguero, Kathleen.
PS615.E27  1989        811'.5'08         88-27868
ISBN 0-8203-1122-7 (alk. paper)
ISBN 0-8203-1123-5 (pbk.: alk. paper)

British Library Cataloging in Publication Data available

To all poets, whatever their traditions, who celebrate the diversity of American experience

# Contents

# Preface

*An Ear to the Ground* is a collection of poems that affirms the richness and cultural complexity of contemporary poetry in the United States. It is an anthology that abandons the myopic notion of center (European, male literary tradition) and periphery (all other cultural influences) in favor of the more accurate representation of contemporary U.S. literature. As Geoffrey O'Brien wrote in the *Voice Literary Supplement* (July 1985), "A poetry anthology is a map, and hence exerts a disproportionate influence: what country you end up in depends on the scope and clarity of the available charts." Our maps are out of date and lead us over and over the same terrain. We hope to begin to chart not new territory, but a land that has too long gone unmapped. This collection demonstrates what a 'literature of inclusion' might comprise, indeed what *must* comprise any anthology purporting accurately to represent a contemporary U.S. poetry which, as Fred Moramarco has noted, "is as vast as the continent, as various as its inhabitants" (*American Book Review*, vol. 9, no. 5). We have brought together the work of a rich and diverse group of poets. Some have been writing since early in this century, others are young. Some of them are little known, others are well known yet still often overlooked in the general canon. *A Gift of Tongues: Critical Challenges in Contemporary American Poetry* (University of Georgia Press, 1987) proposes a critical basis for such an anthology, exploring the ways aesthetics and culture are related. But, although the poetry treated in that volume can be tracked down in little magazines and small presses, no collection exists of such diverse work in a single volume. *An Ear to the Ground* presents the work of many of the poets discussed in the critical essays as well as others who together represent this country's multicultural poetry. These are artists whose historical and literary presence has been ignored or denied altogether. For instance, while the influence of Japanese poetry is clear and acknowledged in the work of American poets such as Gary Snyder or Kenneth Rexroth, Japanese American poetry has gained little critical recognition. Similarly, Latin American poets from Pablo Neruda to Octavio Paz to Cesar Vallejo have been widely translated, taught, and emulated while Chicano or Puerto Rican writers remain without a wide audience.

Critical attention is determined for the most part in the university. And still in this country, the university professor is most often trained to the male, white bourgeois culture, and likely to perpetuate that culture at the expense of the others that inform our national reality. We have, then, a literature of exclusion. "There is," as Adrian Oktenberg notes, "a great silence where . . . art created by the common people ought to be" (A *Gift of Tongues*, p. 85). Such silence, of course, impoverishes our literature and, even more insidiously, tends to invalidate the experience of those it excludes. Richard Oyama describes the effect of the silence: "Because our history was not told in textbooks and our writers were not even mentioned in literature classes, for a long time I felt that my own experience was outside history" (A *Gift of Tongues*, p. 249). Writer Quincy Troupe asserts, "This kind of thing is not a mistake. It's done either by design or because of the way people are taught: they just don't think about certain things—such as that black Americans are American" (quoted by Debbie Mayer in "Is There a Poetry Mafia?" *Coda*, 1981).

Ironically, the male, white bourgeois cultural tradition of individual heroism is little more than a model for self doubt. Some of those counted among its finest practitioners, such as John Berryman or T. S. Eliot, end their search for self in personal or social despair, finding the modern world mediocre or trivial. On the other hand, those excluded from that tradition must painfully reconstruct their own histories: "you see, I too scan / storefront windows / to verify I exist . . ." (Bob Henry Baber, "handicaps"). And they often find themselves fallen between cultures: "Girl, I say / it is dangerous to be a woman of two countries (Linda Hogan, "The Truth Is"). Lorna Dee Cervantes writes of being in Mexico: "I don't want to pretend I know more / and can speak all the names. I can't," and of being in Washington, "I don't belong this far north" ("Visions of Mexico while at a Writing Symposium in Port Townsend Washington"). Annette Kolodny speaks of "the woman poet's repeated need to assert for herself some validating female tradition and to repossess its voices for her own needs" (A *Gift of Tongues*, p. 122). In repossessing their histories in all their complexities, the poets here have created a rich and positive poetics of empowerment. To quote Lorna Dee Cervantes once more, "The best of what I am / is in the gravel behind the train yard / where obsidian chips lodge / in the rocks like beetles. / I burrow and glow" ("Beetles").

To have a collective historical awareness and an appreciation of cultural differences, we need "a shared public forum, some means through which disparate voices can address, or confront, one another" (Sven Birkerts, "Poetry and Politics," *Margin 4*, Autumn 1987). *An Ear to the Ground* presents one kind of forum. The poets write not only out of personal concerns, but from particular cultural histories with a sense of community and social context. Their notions of the nature and functions of art may differ from those enshrined by the academy. Their work may be unfamiliar in its assumptions, traditions, use of language or choices of subject matter. Their poems grow from experiences and stories other than those that have dominated the classroom textbooks. As Margaret Atwood writes, "a language is not words only, / it is the stories / that are told in it, / the stories that are never told" ("Four Small Elegies," *Two Headed Poems*, Simon and Schuster, 1978). David Mura, in his unpublished essay "Notes for a New Poem," examines the effect suppression has had on contemporary writers in the United States:

> Witnessing such erasures, we find it harder and harder to condone any forgetting, any desire to make things simple and whole, to smooth over the narrative. And we find it harder to praise a peace which leaves out our suffering, our vanished voices. A Native American who looks at the fields of the Dakotas finds it hard to forget how that land was stolen. When I look at pictures of Heart Mountain standing over a relocation camp, I find I cannot just rest in the beauty of nature. A southern black looking at the cotton fields in Mississippi remembers the years of slave labor. . . . It seems extremely difficult for people like this to say, "A field can, at times, be just a field."

These poets are asking the reader to look again, look deeper into the history of this country to understand better its present. They write, Mura says, to "restore the strangeness to history, to recover its otherness." Their poems are political acts if politics can be understood to mean "that process whereby we transcend our self-enclosed condition; language is the tool we have evolved for accomplishing this" (Sven Birkerts, ibid.). But language can be used against as well as for its citizens. As Lonny Kaneko describes a first grade teacher, "The words are always hers. She draws / the list and keeps the rules." And, later in the poem, ". . . enemy! I've mixed / American and Japanese" (from "Bailey Gatzert: The First Grade, 1945").

It is not in our common interest to pretend that a single voice speaks for all our citizens or that the language we use is static. English in the United States echoes with the words and inflections of every immigrant and native population. Our history is not one of personages but of people, and the language of our people is dense with reference. Black poetry, writes Raymond Patterson, stems from a "literary tradition rooted in Africa but growing from the first utterances of African slaves on American shores through their songs and shouts, their stories, their patterns of expression . . . a tradition that allows for a continuity rich in variety and promise" (A *Gift of Tongues*, p. 142). Puerto Rican and Chicano poetry incorporate Spanish phrases into English doing "something to the language that was not there before" (Roberto Marquez, quoted in A *Gift of Tongues*, p. 258). Some Asian words have become common coin in English. To appreciate the possibilities such diversity presents, we need the opportunity to abandon narrow definitions and limiting assumptions and evaluate the poem from the inside out without comparing one tradition to another or judging against an artificially imposed single standard. "For the central issue is not which is 'better,' but what we mean by 'better'" (Paul Lauter, A *Gift of Tongues*, p. 66).

The poems themselves give clues as to how they might be read. Some poets teach the reader how to translate language: "brick meant tarpaper, / fireplace meant wood stove. / And this is why we came to love / the double negative" (Vern Rutsala, "Words"). Some ask us to learn another culture: "we are tong yan, / american born / and immigrants / living in l.a., arizona . . ." (Kitty Tsui, "Don't Let Them Chip Away at Our Language"). And some poets, like Alma Villanueva in her poem "The Harvest," suggest a powerful collaboration between writer and reader:

> A man in jail
> must imagine the
> Earth or go
> crazy. A woman
> in her ninth
> month, her child,
> and I,
> my voice: I
> imagine you listening
> there among the
> stones, gathering
> rainbows.

Villanueva not only trusts her voice, she *creates* an audience who can hear what she is saying. As the scope of our attention widens, we will hear more and more. It is our intent not only to enlarge the possibilities of a contemporary poetry canon, but to speak to an audience that already exists: an audience, as Quincy Troupe describes it, that is "the largest in America." It is all of us.

Acknowledging that our own backgrounds and education have not been without bias, we have tried to present what we judge the best of many aesthetics rather than those that necessarily match our own. In this we were assisted by recommendations from other writers and critics, as well as by our own research and reading over the years. We have included wherever possible the work of poets discussed in *A Gift of Tongues*, and augmented that list with the work of other poets who ought properly be included in any general consideration of contemporary U.S. poetry.

Although the essays in *A Gift of Tongues* explore the ways in which aesthetics are related to cultural backgrounds, and although many of our poets do write out of their particular heritages, we did not consciously select their most "ethnic" work for *An Ear to the Ground*. Similarly, recognizing the complexities of their concerns and appeal, we have presented the poets in alphabetical order because we prefer to give the poems the first say. We have provided brief biographical notes and a bibliography.

We are aware that we have undertaken a task that, in its ambition, is destined to fall short. There could easily be a dozen such anthologies (and we hope there will be). We cannot pretend to redress generations of misperception and omission. But, as Lynda Koolish writes, "if imagining a changed world will not cause it to come into being, we know the consequences of failing to imagine it" (*A Gift of Tongues*, p. 14). This anthology is meant to be an invitation to such imaginings. It is a tribute to a vigorous and vital U.S. poetry that speaks to and for its own people and which has the courage to address the world.

Marie Harris
Kathleen Aguero
1989

# Acknowledgments

All poems in this book are copyrighted in the name of the author unless otherwise specified.

Steve Abbott: "Elegy" and "Hit by a Space Station" from *Stretching the Agape Bra* (Androgyne Press), © 1980 by Steve Abbott. Reprinted by permission of the author.

Paula Gunn Allen: "Taku skanskan" and "Molly Brant, Iroquois Matron, Speaks" from *Skin and Bones* (West End Press, 1988).

Maggie Anderson: "To Carry All of Us," "Spitting in the Leaves," and "Among Elms and Maples, Morgantown, West Virginia, August 1935" from *Cold Comfort* (University of Pittsburgh Press), © 1986 by Maggie Anderson. Reprinted by permission of the University of Pittsburgh Press.

Antler: "Bedrock Mortar Full Moon Illumination" and "Raising My Hand" from *Last Words* (Ballantine Books, Available Press), © 1986 by Antler. Reprinted by permission of the author.

Bob Arnold: "The Skin of Her Neck," "Real Life," and "Ghosts" from *Cache* (Mad River Press), © 1987 by Bob Arnold. "Real Life" also appeared in *Country Journal* (July 1980). "Ghosts" appeared in *Ploughshares*, vol. 8, nos. 2–3. Reprinted by permission of the author.

# An Ear to the Ground

# Steve Abbott

## Elegy

The first timepieces were encased in delicate silver skulls.
*Memento mori.* You may smile to hear this
since much of what we say is gallows humor. We would die laughing
but time encases us both as we are young & healthy.
It was not always so. I recall floating up
from one wrinkled corpse with total delight. It was maybe
the 16th century & I fled into exile to escape the stake.
First goes sight, then hearing, touch, taste & finally smell;
so say the Tibetan monks who wrote their Book of the Dead.
Whether fire, loneliness or love hurts more than death I don't
know but I'm reminded of driving 14 hours to Key West
& lying beside you only to hallucinate your beautiful face
a grinning skull. I lost the poem that told of this.
When I lost my first lover, murdered by an AWOL Marine,
I drove round all night howling helplessly
yet no one could hear me. The windows were up. Before my wife
died, she dreamt of our fishtank breaking & all the fish
flopping into the street. No one would help her save them.
She was a psychologist & fell in love with a psychotic patient,
a kid who wanted to kill everyone in a small town. He was
fantastic in bed. Altho he hated queers he imagined me
coming toward him like Jesus with a garland of roses on my head.
I knew this boded ill fortune.

                         The dead
communicate to us in strange ways, or is it only because it is so
ordinary we think it strange. I don a dark suit & wear a white veil,
pretend I'm a monastery prefect reading the Cloud of Unknowing.
The top of my head floats effortlessly into past or future perfect.
An ancestor of Virginia Woolf, one James Pattle, was put in a cask of spirits
when he died & thus shipped back to his wife. She went crazy. It's difficult
to conceive what the Black Death meant to 14th century Europe. That
    Hebrew
tribes & Roman Legions massacred whole cities is generally forgotten

1

but then so too Auschwitz. Life is bleak enough
under the best of conditions. I wonder if a book of poems has ever
been written about murderers. If not, I'd like to write one.
Caligula, Justinian—one could do volumes on the late Roman Emperors
    alone
But what is more terrible than the death of one child?
The last poem would be about Dan White, the Twinkie killer,
& his love for green Ireland. It's terrible beauty.
When I learned my wife's skull was crushed by a truck, my head
swam like an hourglass into a tv set. All the channels went crazy.
Crickets sounded like Halloween noisemakers & I remember explaining the
    event
to our 2 year old daughter with the aid of her Babar book.
Babar's mother was shot by a mean hunter & that makes Alysia sad even
    now.
We distance ourselves for protection, wear scarves when it's cold.
What seems most outlandish in our autobiography is what really happened.
It is only circumstances that make death a terrible event.
She dreamt of our fishtank breaking & all the fish . . .
You should not have to burn your hand everyday to feel the mystery of fire.


## Hit by a Space Station

Certain events are not unlike new snow
but fall as children waking up from dream.
Such it was when I met you. A space
station might thus have fallen upon us.
We wore expressions of perpetual surprise
that we could still be moved by love.

O much maligned Uranians in love,
this age would fling us aside as dirty snow.
That we produce is cause for surprise.
It's said we live in a world of twisted dream
and this is not the least complaint against us.
Yet our hearts melt into vast and empty space

somehow creating a new order of space;
a healing place for nature, our falling in love,

2

which flows, surges, takes meaning beyond us.
Like maple sap rising above snow
we rise above cold dogmatic dream
into the sunny music of surprise.

We wear expressions of perpetual surprise
that many cannot comprehend this space.
Might aliens in UFO's dream
preferable variants of love?
Love frolics as children in fresh snow—
an unexpected wonder between any of us.

So too, protons and electrons charge inside us.
That they dance at all is the surprise
that stops us cold as sudden snow.
Scary too, as falling. But to space
into rigid rules all ways of love
would kill the nucleus, the very heart of dream.

The time has come we must defend our dream,
proclaim *this* as what is best in us.
Where would we be without our variant love?
The world would shrivel, die. Without surprise
boredom would be the sole master of space
and summer joys would perish under constant snow.

Releasing dream we shower the world with surprise
spontaneous as light. We redeem this space
as satellites orbiting dead snow.

## Taku skanskan

that history is an event
that life is
that I am event
usually to go do something
the metaphor for god.
eventuality.
activity.

what happens      *to be*
what happens      *to me*
god.      history.      action
the Lakota word for it is:
whatmovesmoves.
they don't call god "what moves something."
not "prime mover."
"first mover" "who moves everything or nothing"
"action." "lights." "movement."
not "where" or "what" or "how" but
event.      GOD
is what happens, is:
movesmoves.

riding a mare.
eventuality.
out of the corral into morning
taking her saddled and bridled
air thick with breath movesmoves
horsebreath, mybreath, earthbreath
skybreathing air.      ing.
breathesbreathes      movesmoves
in the cold.      winterspringfall.
corral.      ing.      horse and breath.
air.      through the gate moveswe.
lift we the wooden crossbar *niya*

movesmoves unlocks movesbreathes
lifebreath of winter soul
swings wide sweet corral gate
happens to be frozenstiff in place
happens to be cold.    so I and mare
wear clothes thatmove in event
of frozen. shaggydressers for the air that
breathes breathe we: flows: movesmoves:
god its cold.
no other place but movemove
horse me gate hinge air bright frost lungs burst
swing gate far morning winter air rides
movesmovingmoves    Lakotas say: god.
what we do.

## Molly Brant, Iroquois Matron, Speaks

> I was, Sir, born of Indian parents, and lived while a child among those
> whom you are pleased to call savages; I was afterwards sent to live
> among the white people, and educated at one of your schools; . . . and
> after every exertion to divest myself of prejudice, I am obliged to give my
> opinion in favor of my own people. . . . In the government you call civi-
> lized, the happiness of the people is constantly sacrificed to the splendor
> of empire. . . .
>
> Joseph Brant

We knew it was the end
long after it ended, my brother Joseph
and I. We were so simple in those days
taking a holiday to see the war,
the one they would later call
the Revolution. It was that,
at that. Something turned,
something was revolting.
And when I learned that I was
no longer honored matron
but only heathen squaw,
when I learned my daughters
were less than dirt,
then I knew that it was changed,

and our lives were ended.
I wonder why I did not see it coming
all along.

It's a funny thing about revolutions.
Wheels turn. So do planets.
Stars turn. So do galaxies.
What's odd is that when a human
system turns, so many believe
it will turn their way.
So many think any turn is for the better.
I suppose we thought so,
my brother Joseph and myself.
I suppose we thought that if the whites
were fighting we Iroquois couldn't help
but come out ahead. We had held power
for so long. We played the international
political game to our advantage
for two hundred years—
seemed like we had always had
our way in things. Seemed like
we always would. The Matrons had held
power for so long—for as long as anyone
could remember—how could we know
the turn events would take, the turn
that would plow us under
like last year's crop?

And now another turn is up.
They plan to blow it up.
Or poison it to death rather than change.
Fire and poison, their own tools
of conquest will conquer them, it seems.
They want revolution,
but not that kind, I guess,
any more than we hoped for
the kind of revolution that we got.
So they are planning to blow it up,
obliterate it. And good riddance
is what I say. What do I have to lose,
having lost all that mattered, all I loved

so long ago? And what is there more to lose?
Great cities, piling drifting clouds
of chemical poisons that have long since
killed the air? Rivers and lakes long since
dead beneath the burden of filth dumped into
them for years? Earth so sick of attempts
to cure it of its life that it is nearly dead?
Places now called Oregon, California, New York,
filled with those who replaced the people
long since murdered in the revolution
that turned the red lands white?
If death is in the wind
it will only blow our enemies away.
When a wheel turns
what is on the underside
comes up.

# alurista

## miami rastas

rastafarians in miami speak
in perfect caribbean spanish
rats roam the streets and many
taxi drivers look like z. acosta
the coast is still part of thee
mexican gulf, in spite mon
the gusano arrogance and boot
or marielito malice and Blades
a debt remains true, Rubén
solid as a day dream drum
dark rum eyed eyed child
ivory teeth power smile
even the germans sprechen
blurting explosive cervantinian
verbos in this here nether
ever, neverland peninsula
of glades, blades, slaves
this beach and the bananos
this city and the zealous guard
a nightmare lost to an epiphanous
windmill full of dice and eyes
windmill full of ice and rice and
not payable; nyet, not collectable either
pa'que tu sepa', inform thyself, b él

## southwestern trek in four part harmony

first movement

could i have a dollar?
the sun peaks
behind the camera focusing

8

to capture those raisin, black sun
almond eyes and hustling grin
. . . an old man at the age of seven
dark clouds cloak the sky
i wear a saguryo mexican hat
little floyd asks then
if he can have my "stetson"
. . . "u can keep the feathers
. . . i got some myself"
our heads r roughly the same size
so r our feet
. . . "i'll trade it for your boots"
i say to him with a smirk
. . . "it's gonna drizzle tonight"
little floyd whittles out and
disappears on the dust of
his rebuilt huffy bike


                second movement

. . . "oh, those wonderful, wonnnderful kids,"
one says with gleeful superficiality
"they remind me of my nephews"
—i bet your nephews
wouldn't come up to a stranger
and ask for a dollar
. . . "oh no, they wouldn't"
she snaps back with self-importance
—do u know why they wouln't?
. . . "well, *they* were raised
by two schoolteachers"
—you're equivocating, i say to her
carefully and ironically enunciating
the sunday word i'm hurling
. . . "i beg your pardon!
—*they* wouldn't go up to a complete
stranger and ask for a dollar
because *they have* a dollar, or two . . .
briskly she walks away clutching
her recently acquired squash blossom

sterling cast necklace to her heart
inside the pueblo mission a lecture awaits
myth is easier to handle than *class*


## third movement

it wasn't hard to find my spot
a small clearing surrounded
by piñon trees glowed with
my colors, the hues were friendly
the dusk was more like ashes
than it was embers or the crack
between two worlds, the campfire
crackled with murmured voices
rain clouds hovered around
the zuñi mountains' mesquite
rain trickled gently and warm
this evening, this very dew
exactly forty years after
the first A bomb test
white sands remains a ghost
white house still posits
"limited nuclear warfare"
as a plausible "defense"
the piñon knows naught


## fourth movement

. . . "grasshopper," xaolín master
whispered thunder, "when in
search for epiphany in aztlán,
make sure u leave some stones
unturned. these may b radioactive
make heads roll and fall out
when they broadcast about others
what they emanate themselves

ZAZ! ! ! ! !

# Maggie Anderson

## To Carry All of Us

Only responsible people keep cows. If you buy near cattle,
you can count on your neighbors to be home repairing fences.
Cows don't know how much they cost, or yield, and cats
are free. I always cried, as a child, when we drove
past the stockyard and had to hear the cattle, moaning
because crowded, not knowing they were going to die.
It's still their ignorance that breaks my heart.

How elaborately the savings of the desperate poor pile up:
old car parts and empty bottles, broken dolls and rusty
buckets hung on nails, and always cats, who seek the indigent
out. As a child, I preferred the littered farms,
where, it seemed to me, the accumulation
was, like art, arranged by some design.

And as a child, I'd be horse to my friend Patty
with her brace and orthopedic shoe. A rope around my waist,
I'd gallop easy so Patty could keep up and we'd run
to the hilltop to see all the farms. Once, a bearded woman
in overalls and army jacket, screamed at us to get away
from her collected bounty spreading out from the porch
to her unposted fields. She spooked the cattle
next farm over, and they took off so their hooves
shook the ground where we stood. I took off too
and Patty tugged my rope, but I was wild enough
to carry her despite her limp. I was wild and strong enough
to carry all of us. I could be a bearded woman on a porch
and still have cows and not care how I dressed. I could
yell at little girls who pretended to be horses, save
everything that ever came to me: all my cats lined up
on tidy fences, my cattle never slaughtered for money.

## Spitting in the Leaves

In Spanishburg there are boys in tight jeans,
mud on their cowboy boots and they wear huge hats
with feathers, skunk feathers they tell me.
They do not want to be in school, but are.
Some teacher cared enough to hold them. Unlike
their thin disheveled cousins, the boys on Matoaka's
Main Street in October who loll against parking meters
and spit into the leaves. Because of them, someone
will think we need a war, will think the best solution
would be for them to take their hats and feathers,
their good country manners and drag them off somewhere,
to Vietnam, to El Salvador. And they'll go.
They'll go from West Virginia, from hills and back roads
that twist like politics through trees, and they'll fight,
not because they know what for but because what they know
is how to fight. What they know is feathers,
their strong skinny arms, their spitting
in the leaves.

## Among Elms and Maples, Morgantown, West Virginia, August 1935

Houses are wedged between the tall stacks
of Seneca Glass beside the Monongahela
and waffle up steep hills. Here, the terrain
allows photographers to appear acrobatic.
Walker Evans liked standing on a hill, focusing
down so it seemed he was poised on a branch.
He liked the single telephone pole against
the flat sky, crossed off-center like a crucifix.
Beneath it, among elms and maples, is the house
my mother lived in with her sister and their mother
nearly fifty years ago. In this shot, Evans
only wanted the rough surfaces of clapboard
houses, their meshed roofs and slanted gables.
He didn't want my mother peeling the thin skin

from tomatoes with a sharp knife, my clumsy
Aunt Grace chasing the ones she'd dropped
around the linoleum floor. That would be another
picture, not this one. I look back from the future,
past the undulating, unremitting line of hills
Evans framed my family in, through the shaggy fronds
of summer ferns he used as foreground and as border.

## Bedrock Mortar Full Moon Illumination

Seeing the reflection of the full moon
    in the rainfilled bedrock mortar holes
        where earliest California Indians
    ground acorns with circular grinding stones
And sensing how the full moon
    is like a mortar stone in the sky,
And then seeing the image of my face
    looking up at me from the moonlit surface
        and sensing my own evanescence,
    how my face is like an acorn
        time grinds to fine dust,
And thinking thousands of years
    Indians ground acorns here
Singing their acorn songs
    gossipping and laughing
        or silent and musing
    listening to the pleasing sound
        of mortar stones grinding acorns
Or after a big storm
    gazing in the rainfilled holes
        at their reflections
    or seeing the full moon mirrored
Or deer hot from play
    dipping shy twilight muzzles
        in the cool pools
As blue oak and black oak
    ponderosa pine and digger pine
        incense cedar and manzanita
    grew and died in continuous
        ever-changing spots
    around the site.
Yet just as surely years from now
    faces staring here

After scooping out fallen leaves
    and feeling with future fingers
        the wet smooth tapering holes
    in the mossy lichen-covered rock
        contemplating themselves
    looking up at themselves
        contemplating these same thoughts
    will vanish,
While century after century the full moon
    continues to stare down
        and see its face
    unseen by anyone in the forest
Reflected in the rainfilled mortar holes
    from long ago.


## Raising My Hand

One of the first things we learn in school is
    if we know the answer to a question
We must raise our hand and be called on
    before we can speak.
How strange it seemed to me then,
    raising my hand to be called on,
How at first I just blurted out,
    but that was not permitted.

How often I knew the answer
And the teacher (knowing I knew)
Called on others I knew (and she knew)
    had it wrong!
How I'd stretch my arm
    as if it would break free
    and shoot through the roof
    like a rocket!
How I'd wave and groan and sigh,
Even hold up my aching arm
    with my other hand
Begging to be called on,

Please, *me*, I know the answer!
Almost leaping from my seat
    hoping to hear my name.

Twenty-nine now, alone in the wilds,
Seated on some rocky outcrop
    under all the stars,
I find myself raising my hand
    as I did in first grade
Mimicking the excitement
    and expectancy felt then,
No one calls on me
    but the wind.

# Bob Arnold

## The Skin of Her Neck

Tonight, because her hand
Is in pain, the small finger
Swollen, yes, I'll stir the
Batter, although she is better
And first taught me how
Something is done right.
And I came from behind
And smelled the skin of
Her neck, the long blonde
Hairs alive and the blouse
White and rough, tucked into
A thin summer skirt.
Winter, near Christmas,
3 feet of snow and her
Body moves across the
Cabin room with summer,
A clay bowl with
Colored striped in her
Arms, the fresh heat
Of the flat iron stove.

## Real Life

It was a hot day thrown suddenly cool
By that hard rain, poured off the slate roof barn
When the boy was hit by lightning.
Standing safe, he thought, in the large doorway,
Eaves above him tapping,
Farm trucks shining up.
Big for his age, father's overalls, watching things,
Whole complexion tan like pure maple syrup,

17

The stuff he gathered with his grandfather and horses.
His old man and older brothers stoke and boil the woodfire,
Spend those long nights in the sugar house.
The way the light spills out of the small steamy windows
All over the snow, dreamy in the valley.

Well a mean bolt came down from the sky to end that,
A splitting axe flying.
Water dripping smooth from the roof edge
Splashes onto his boots and cuffs,
Hayseed still itching his back,
Cows poking behind him in their stalls,
Need a light already it's getting so dark, he thought—
Struck him from the forehead straight down,
Cracked him open like nothing should be.
The family dog lay nearby on a broken bale
Like he has for 15 Julys,
His large head on his paws, tilted and watching
Rain burning the ground.

## Ghosts

March comes and water moves,
The river, ponds, brooks open.
On snowshoes this is the last week
You'll hike down these banks of
Rotten snow, the last week bridges
Of ice will be there to criss-cross
Down stream, the last week the
Deer carcass will be pinned between
Rocks and white water spray through
The white of her skull—the runoff
Will let her go, or break her to pieces—
You're aware of this where you step.
Pools of water swirl 5 feet deep,
Maybe her bones will lie down in the
Sand and white pebbles here, it is

The last week to think of any of this.
Beneath your feet of oblong ashwood
And softened leather you sense the newness
Of life—hide has slipped all winter off
The body, it is time to go places.

# Russell Atkins

## Trainyard at Night

TH UN DER    TH UN DER
the huge bold blasts black
hiss insists upon hissing insists
on insisting on hissing hiss
hiss s sss ss sss sss ssss s
ss sssss ssss
when whoosh!
the sharp scrap making its fourth lap
with a lot of rattletrap
and slap rap and crap—
I listen in time to hear coming on
the great Limited
it rolls scrolls of fold of fold
like one traditionally old
coldly, meanwhile hiss hiss
hiss insists upon hissing insists
on insisting on hissing hiss
hiss s ss ss sss sss s
sss s s
s

## On the Fine Arts Garden, Cleveland

   The Park's beautiful
                              really
something so serious about it
serene and gloomy
                          mildly gloomy
mildly touching, all things
                            softly
and pouring with
mellows the silver fountain
                                silent figures

20

move reposefully into the living shadows
and then the golden lamps
the while
          slowly filtering—


## Late Bus (After a Series of Hold-Ups)

Theft's hour—the bus
against the hark lights
affright from houses!
Two dark men board laughing
(their teeth, crooked)
and take a seat in back,
two men in jeans, jackets!

the bus blunders on, bounced
(the streets are deserted)
          —we wait
the men sit     still:
they say nothing,
yeah—their eyes (—sure,
we know what's up—)
one *feigns* awhile of sleep,
one coughs quickly as a signal
while the other holds—now!
—is it now?!
          watch their pockets,
their hands are moving,
one, as for a cigarette
and one *as if* finding
matches
     he reaches, reaches up
—falsely?—to pull the bell
cord               East 55
they leave the bus

it makes no difference:
*four* dark men board
          laughing

# bob henry baber

## Richwood

Once I was a grape nehi
to the woodhicks standing on the porch of the Sportsmen
chewing mail pouch tobacco
and spitting into a Heinz pork and beans can . . .

Just a stripling really—
green and tender as a yearling—
all ears and crewcut and jughead
sent on a mission of milk
but waylaid by words
and stories of wildcats and blizzards
skid roads and timber it took four tries
with a six foot cross cut
to lay down

on hot days when pulp swelled with puberty
I absorbed the woodgrain of men
who with horses stretched sinews in mud and work—
who dug brogan heels into mountains and shale
and grunted together like primal lovers in suffering sweat;
who filled their nostrils with fog and laurel thickets,
woodsmoke and fresh cut oak;
whose tongues grew fat with Karo syrup
thick as spring sap on biscuits;
who stripped naked and laid down in Laurel Crick,
bathed themselves inside and out with moonshine
and gathered pollen from bodies of young women
sweeter than wild honeysuckle,
who scattered seeds over these hills
that sprouted and prospered safely beneath their canopy . . .

but now, with the stumps of ancient snags
rotting at my base,

I stand alone in sweetwater and sun
spiraling into an empty sky,
my roots sunk deep into humus, leafmold, and regrets,
richer, for what once thrived here, than death itself.


## handicaps

With their stares others tell me
what I already know to be the truth:
my features do not conform
to the conventions of beauty or grace
When I hurry across Capital
with its unforgiving light
my feet and arms fail me,
and when I speak
my thoughts, though clear,
are slush as much as ice—
Still I say the difference between us
is only that of form.
You see, I too scan storefront windows
to verify I exist;
I too am stunned by the polluted sunset
like a gash in skyscraper glass;
I too hear the churchbells
ringing in the early orange dusk;
I envy youth its poetry
and its unrelenting lust

and my breath, like yours—
warm, humid, and grey—
lifts from deep within my lungs
pauses in December air
and evaporates
          as we all must
        in our sad anointed time
        in our difference of like, not kind

# Jimmy Santiago Baca

## Ese Chicano

Behind bars you stand
peering down into the cellblock landing
where porters mill,
leaning on mops and brooms.

You wear dark sunglasses
like your Indio ancestors
wore black war paint.

Christ crucified across your chest,
a dragon on your left arm,
rose trellis on your right arm,
Virgen de Guadalupe on your back.

Believer of blood duels.
You believe someday
the earth will crack, and Aztecas will rise
from the dead.

You whistle like a bird
in the steel branches of bars
at a friend across the cellblock,
asking secretly with your hands
if he has something to quench the thirst
of the vines
growing around your arms,

so that the secret flower of your heart
may sleep.

## I Pass La Iglesia

I pass la iglesia, then back up
and climb up the steps to the landing
and look in. An old viejo kneels in front
of la virgen, beckoning her to remove
the boulder from his heart. I lean
against the great doors watching.

The candles at her feet like flaming guards
swing their silvery sabers
in front of his brown eyes, warm intimate creatures
that ask forgiveness from the mysterious marble.

It's December and he has a gray coat on.
He makes the sign of the cross
and slowly rises. The altar behind him,
thorn-studded slits of flame in blue and red candle jars
spring and twist like a net
wrestling with some invisible wild dog.


## Small Farmer

"Yessum, I'm a small farmer.
Don't know iffen I can make it
another year. Tain't good, tain't good atall."

The flute of a tractor
plays to the bones of the old farmer,
reveals a history
chaptered with warm and cold weather.

"Look deez cobby hands
smeared with bug blood and dirt
on my dried corn stalk arms. Stills,
I yearns fo rain in my slow movements."

Blades drag and plough her weed shag,
turn fresh mother saps

25

to both sides earth piles. He calls it
"the cool dark meat of crops."

So the field bleeds up-turned naked dirt.
I ask him, what do you believe in?
"I take a seed between my thumb and finger,
I crack, crawl into it
and make my life from there."

"I think like an insect
sun drunk and cackling wings
at their green tables of leaves,
poison them with my insecticide."

The field changes form,
a young girl kicking up dirt
in a green dress. Her perfume
fills your nostrils.

On your knees you rub her loins,
your hands in the cool dark mounds
like roots: she giggles green tongues,
whispering leaves unfold their secrets to you.

Woman now, everywhere
her green waist waving with lust.
Tottering with age in your khaki pants and shirt,
you take her, face bright with sweat.

With each yank at the corn stalks she grunts.
Your hand reaches under her clothing
closing and opening
on the warm corn and sweet potatoes.

# Robin Becker

## Living in the Barn

*For Marianne Weil*

Beside you in the truck, I almost forget
you are a woman, thirty, turning the wheel,
slamming the door. You could be a boy, fifteen,
slim and eager for exercise in a soiled shirt and jeans.
By the time you closed the deal, the animals were gone,
but their ghosts raise their heads as we pass.
Black and white cows reclaim the pasture; curious billygoats
eye two women rattling up the drive. Like an archetypal barn
from memory, the barn slumps broad and red in the rain.
Now the great hayloft holds your bed and table.
In dreams, the farm boys bale and hurl their burdens
into the atrium; I feel the heavy hooves of Clydesdales
stamping in their stalls; the walls still hold their scent,
their hairs, their troughs, their significant sighs.

You have restored yourself by restoring this barn—
long days under the sun's hot hand,
hours at the drafting table—
planning for the time you would have what you need:
a place to work, a place to live.
Like barnswallows high in the rafters,
your sculptures float and fly, wings beating against weathered wood.
In the studio, your welding tools assume the shapes
of fantastic creatures, the bronze and brass of your trade.
You lace your boots, tie back your hair,
prepare for work like a farmer whose animals,
like a ring of friends, surround him.

## Medical Science

My father's heart is on television
at the hospital. Lonely and a little embarrassed, it beats blindly on
the videotape, hoping for the best. Like family
members of a game-show contestant, my mother and I stand off
to the side, proud of the healthy culvert doing its chores.
The doctor explains that this is the artery of
a much younger man, and I think of the parts of my father's
body assembled in a shop from the odds and ends
of others. Now the doctor
is speaking very quickly, as if she could hide
the sad blocked door of the right
ventricle, unable to pass its burden of blood
from one room to another. When the lights go on, I
expect to see it, sore and swollen, counting
off the seconds with its bad arm. My mother
takes a few steps, respectfully, holding her
pocketbook, waiting to be addressed. We have seen
the unshaven face of the heart, the cataract
eyes of the heart, the liver-spotted hands
of the heart. Seated in the cafeteria, my mother whispers
that my father's heart is a miracle, that it has already been dead
and recalled twice.


## Dangers

I've never understood love,
how it grows between people like good grass
and how you must keep clearing
a larger space for it
until your lover has a field
so large she is free
as a white-tailed deer roaming
the southwestern mountains.

In the mountains
the air is so thin my friend
stops lightheaded on the path

28

and then we go on, pausing
to let our words catch up with us.
Because we are friends
the small streams and rocks
are always interesting,

and our stories reveal
not only failures of nerve but moments
when we held the hand of someone dying
and released it and found ourselves
in the country of grieving. The air, though dangerous,
is a small danger; the larger ones we shun together,
sure only of the marked trail,
the names of a few birds, the way down.

# Duane Big Eagle

## My Socks Are Thin

My socks are thin.
My feet are like bones
tapping the taut skin of a drum.
My trousers dance by themselves
holding me up.
My shirt balloons with emptiness.
I'm about to be taken away
from my sheath of darkness,
my quiet inner musing.
My hands mechanically grapple,
logically, repeatedly.
My machine gun eyes
are about to open and raze
the tender shoots of blue grass,
the voluptuous craving for ochre rock.
My ears are about to be filled
with the mud and dung
of commerce, of jealousy,
of the precisely straight line.
I have only a single moment
for my lips,
like fire caressing the page,
to tell you
of salvation and error,
of leisure and love,
of the whirling up from black depths
of song.

## Parisian Streets

1

Distant music
drifts through the window
from the Boulevard Raspail.
I had forgotten
that I would feel
hunger or cold or pain,
forgotten that I would return.
There is no name
for the time
we lay together.
How is it that this house
still stands,
that a light can shine
on steps across the street?
How can these solid bodies
appear and disappear
like distant music
heard through wind?

2

When we met,
I thought nothing
could separate us,
not even distance.
I saw your face
through the glass top
of a restaurant booth
but you'd vanished
when I ran out.
Was it really you?
Circle of silence,
the cement street
and trees.

Common things occupy my mind,
taxi cabs, the sign for the lost and found.
There is no sculpture on this corner
and your face does not appear
in the leaves of trees.

In search of you
I journey a thousand kilometers
into the countryside,
enter a two hundred year old
stone farm house
and hear
Charlie Parker—
"Scrapple from the Apple"
(Radio Jugoslavia).

Valeriano.
Latin, *valere*, to be strong.
News reaches me today
of your birth
many thousands of miles away.
You have fallen
from the woman that I love,
from the ocean of generations,
out of our arms
into turmoil and the world.

The streets, I know, could be anywhere.
The child, I know, is mine and not mine.
I see him for the first time,
feel for a moment
in the last warmth of autumn

a young father feed his son
ice cream in a sidewalk cafe.


7


Morning sunlight
streams in through a wall
where neither door nor window
opens.
Two ravens become
his small eyes.
His childish singing
is the only sound I know,
songs of lost legends
of my ancestors
pressed into the soft earth
of my flesh.

# Karen Brodine

## By Fire or by Water

### 1. February

Dreams this terrible week.

Su and I are standing on an open porch waiting for people
to arrive. In every direction, a pure and fierce and gentle
snow is falling.

I'm dancing a kind of waltz-polka, faster, faster, till I
spin off from my partner, off balance, careening.

A tiny dog yaps at my heels, harassing, then changes to a
green seaweed–covered poodle—dragging at my coat.

won't let me BE.

Someone turns a waterhose full in my face, washes me
down the concrete steps. In the dream I think,
"What did I do to deserve this?"

.     .     .     .     .

Some people act a little funny now, awkward about cancer—
I try to put them at ease with jokes. At times,
the anxiety rises in me like a flood.

.     .     .     .     .

The doctor says that once you have cancer you are followed
by the medical profession for the rest of your life.

.     .     .     .

Wading through brush in the night, a man is following me.
I am not sure if this is by chance or if he menaces.
I turn to study his face. I whip my hands through the air
cutting at the brush to threaten him with how fierce I am.

34

He keeps following. I keep watch, beating at the brush,
wake, gasping. His face is young, square, somewhat
twisted, watching me.

I have seen his face.
He has seen my strength.
Who will win?


## 2. March

When I was a kid someone would say,
ok, what would you choose, death by fire or water?
Pragmatic, I would never play that game. Now I have to.
A new twist, the bribe is life. Life by fire, death
by percentage, life by water, drowning
all your cells just enough.

Remission is disappearance for the time being.
Cure is death by other causes.

My chances for recurrence are 35% without chemo,
half that, with. A clear choice.
Till you add barbarities of treatment. Would you
prefer to chance diabetes or heart failure,
dizziness or seeing halos round the moon?

I've never been the least religious.
Now they're tossing halos round my neck like horseshoes,
and I'm the pole, no angel, stiff and afraid,
arm protective of the missing breast.

What will happen when I swallow the poison?
Which poison should I choose?

Someone flips a coin and here I stand in my body,
one more gamble, one more statistic.

I'm like a boy on one side, a woman on the other.
Doesn't bother me so much, reminds me of running wild
and lithe through the woods, like a colt.

What bothers me is I may lose my lashes,
through which I look, shaded and protected,
at the world.

The dr. says he's biased toward research.
I've got another bias.
The dr. says he can't say what he would advise
if it were his wife or daughter or even himself.
Because he's not in my position.
But what are imaginations for?

Too many times I have imagined my mother, wrestling
with her tardy, errant heart, anchored to that couch
by a failing muscle. Still she came back,
dragging half her body at the leash,
into determined movement and life.


## 3. April

Trying to guide a horse and a lion to safety, yarn about
their necks, hands tangled in their manes. The animals
are wild, want to wander through the woods, directionless.
But we must go toward home. Rough, make-shift tools,
the wild animals of the body. Vigilance, consciousness,
and the ability to fight. Understanding in order to fight.

.    .    .    .    .    .

An evil woman kept changing shape.
She kept striking when I turned my back.
When I looked again, she had taken
all the tires off my car.

I knew it was her because she wore
one earring, icy blue, shaped like a
wind chime, irregular, jagged.

I faced her down.
We stared at one another.
I knew I couldn't look away.

This was a contest and I must not
even blink. We stared and stared
and finally, she changed into a
yolk-like substance and disappeared
into water, dissolved.

I had won, for this moment.

.    .    .    .    .

Trying all angles, everything I can think of,
not giving up, keeping steady in the assault
of the chemo which drains your energy out your
feet till you can't move. I fight the chemo,
more than the cancer.

I don't trust in my weapons entirely.
The cell model helps but it is abstract,
a picture, distant.

The reality is very complex and my mind clamors
to alter it into something concrete,
wicked witches, lions and horses, dogs covered
with seaweed, men stalking me, and me, always,
turning, straining to see, and to
engage in whatever fight is required.

## 4. May

Here, on that new strange plain
where my left breast is no longer
where the angry scar blanches out
to a thin reminder
Here, my heart is closer now
to my lover's ear, listening
to the sun lazing its warm palm
on my pale skin, closer now
to my lover's ear, listening
to the traffic blare

to shouts of street people
to the rasp of each day,
the rough, practical tones.
My heart is closer now.
Hear its steady, stubborn drum.

# Gwendolyn Brooks

## The Near-Johannesburg Boy

*In South Africa the Black*
*children ask each other:*
*"Have you been detained yet?*
*How many times have you been*
*detained?"*

---

*The herein boy does not live*
*in Johannesburg. He is not*
*allowed to live there. Perhaps*
*he lives in Soweto.*

My way is from woe to wonder.
A Black boy near Johannesburg, hot
in the Hot Time.

Those people
do not like Black among the colors.
They do not like our
calling our country ours.
They say our country is not ours.

Those people.
Visiting the world as I visit the world.
Those people.
Their bleach is puckered and cruel.

It is work to speak of my Father. My Father.
His body was whole till they Stopped it.
Suddenly.
With a short shot.
But, before that, physically tall and among us,
he died every day. Every moment.
My Father. . . .

39

First was the crumpling.
No. First was the Fist-and-the-Fury.
Last was the crumpling. It is
a little used rag that is Under, it is not,
it is not my Father gone down.

About my Mother. My Mother
was this loud laugher
below the sunshine, below the starlight at festival.
My Mother is still this loud laugher!
Still moving straight in the Getting-It-Done (as she names it.)
Oh a strong eye is my Mother.
Except when it seems we are lax in our looking.

Well, enough of slump, enough of Old Story.
Like a clean spear of fire
I am moving. I am not still. I am ready
to be ready.
I shall flail
in the Hot Time.

Tonight I walk with
a hundred of playmates to where
the hurt Black of our skin is forbidden.
There, in the dark that is our dark, there,
a-pulse across earth that is our earth, there
there exulting, there Exactly, there redeeming, there
   Roaring Up
(oh my Father)
we shall forge with the Fist-and-the-Fury:
we shall flail in the Hot Time:
we shall
we shall

## Whitney Young

*1921–1971*

Whitney, you were
a candid structure hulking in event.
And you confounded and offended them out there.
They saw you,
arch and precise.
They saw that you were wise, arch, and precise.
They did not like it, Whitney.

We
remark your bright survival over death.
We share your long
comprehension that there is exhilaration
in watching something caught
break free.


## To Those of My Sisters Who Kept Their Naturals

*Never to look
a hot comb in the teeth.*

Sisters!
I love you.
Because you love you.
Because you are erect.
Because you are also bent.
In season, stern, kind.
Crisp, soft—in season.
And you withhold.
And you extend.
And you Step out.
And you go back.
And you extend again.
Your eyes, loud-soft, with crying and
     with smiles,
are older than a million years.

And they are young.
You reach, in season.
You subside, in season.
And All
below the richrough righttime of your hair.
You have not bought Blondine.
You have not hailed the hot-comb recently.
You never worshipped Marilyn Monroe.
You say: Farrah's hair is hers.
You have not wanted to be white.
Nor have you testified to adoration of that
    state
with the advertisement of imitation
(*never* successful because the hot-comb is
    laughing too.)
But oh the rough dark Other music!
the Real,
the Right.
The natural Respect of Self and Seal!
        Sisters!
Your hair is Celebration in the world!

# Joseph Bruchac

## A Fire Story

*Lake George, 1984*

There was just no time
to call for help
out there,
over the hill
from the main blaze
where he had followed
the evening flight
of a spark that might
start it all over,
keep burning for days.

As it got darker,
he circled the fire,
fighting it by its own light,
first from the truck,
then into the brush
with the one-man tank
strapped onto his back.

Feet crunching the char,
he kept spraying the edges,
sparks searing his face
rising up to make stars.

He kept circling in
until all was dark,
as his feet extinguished
one final spark.

That was when
he realized he was lost,
without a flashlight,

no moon in the sky
and all around him
the big woods quiet after
the crack and the whisper of flame.

He knew then
that trouble
is a kind of a marker.
When it's gone,
you can't always
be sure where you are.

Sometimes, when it's over,
all you can do
is just sit in the ashes
and wait for the sun.

## Malsum

Wolf brother, so my old people called you.
Before the missionaries came and named you
brother to the devil, you gave your name
to children, linked our blood to the clan of singers.

From your steps we learned
to walk silent, to choose well which path to take.
As your forests grew smaller, our hearts, too, lost strength.
Your songs were answered by our heartbeats.

Black wolf, bringer of night
you walk by Gluskabe's right side.
White wolf, bringer of day,
you walk by his left.

You teach us how
to raise our children,
stay by our mates and families.

The guns which point
to your hearts point at ours.

You know the old bargain
The Owner made
that you should take those
too weak, too old, too sick to go on,
you should keep the herds clean
of disease, test the strength
of your own people and the hooved ones
until that moment when eyes meet
and the caribou bows its head
one last time

Singer of death,
singer of life,
I want this air
to always share our breaths,
I dream you back into the mountains
and when I cross this river know
as Gluskabe did long ago
I will find you waiting, patient,
on the other side

## Plums

Grandma Bruchac lies with closed eyes,
her hair blue as the skin of a plum,
that color because she washed it before
beginning dinner—the pots were bubbling
on the iron stove when she had the stroke.

In the neatly-made hospital bed
she has slept three days, a traveller
gaining strength before climbing one final hill.
The blue of European plums surrounds

45

her face like flower petals
or fingers stained from picking fruit.

Her face, a pale cloud, drifts further away.
She dreams of Turnava, where the boy
she'll marry years later in this land is waiting.
He has brought her something from his uncle's orchard.
Her hand moves from yours to accept that gift.


## Prayer

Let my words
be bright with animals,
images the flash of a gull's wing.
If we pretend
that we are at the center,
that moles and kingfishers,
eels and coyotes
are at the edge of grace,
then we circle, dead moons
about a cold sun.
This morning I ask only
the blessing of the crayfish,
the beatitude of the birds;
to wear the skin of the bear
in my songs;
to work like a man with my hands.

# David Budbill

## Tommy Again, Finally

Antoine, Doug and Tommy cut logs and pulp right through that winter and
    into spring.
When the black flies came out they gave up working in the woods
and each went his separate way, found summer jobs or no jobs at all.
Tommy went on living with Grace and they both seemed happy as far as
    anybody could tell
and Grace's kids did too.

I saw Grace down to Jerry's Garage once that next spring
and she had a pretty bad shiner,
but nobody said anything about it, and what people thought,
if anything, I can't say.

Then it was summer, the middle of July . . .

Tommy Stames shot himself.

    What? What? What did you say?

Tommy Stames killed himself.

    What did you say?

He shot himself up to his camp.

    Where? Up to his camp?

Up to his camp. Antoine came and got me.

    Tommy Stames killed himself. He shot himself.

Where?

    He killed himself. Up to his camp.

**47**

He left Antoine a note. Antoine came and got me.
All it said was: *Thank you, Antoine.*
                    *You know where to find me.*

He shot himself?

     Antoine came and got me. We went up.
     We brought him back.

Tommy Stames killed himself. He killed himself.

     Tommy went up to his favorite place,
     that little clearing in the woods.

He had a little camp up there, a fireplace,
and a lean-to made of spruce poles and hemlock boughs.
Why, he camped up there.

     And in the lean-to
     there was a book of ancient Chinese poetry

and a Chinese painting
one of those long skinny ones that start down close
and go up
way up far
up into the mountains

     and way up in the mountains in that painting
     there was a little place—

the Chinese called them pavilions,
but it was a lean-to—

     and a man sitting out in front of it,
     just a tiny spot,
     and all alone
     way up in the mountains.

Just like Tommy's place
and just like Tommy.

You go up through the woods, you cross a little stream
and you come to this clearing in the forest
where the light comes in.

Before he killed himself
he made a circle of stones he'd gathered from the stream
and in the circle there were bits of bark and twigs,
little signs or symbols,
something.

You go up through the woods and you cross a little stream.

Antoine came and got me. We went up. We brought him back.

A clearing in the forest where the light comes in.

He camped up there.
It was a little lean-to in the forest.

He put himself in the middle of that circle.
He was sitting down.
He took his army carbine . . .

You go up through the woods.

He left a note for Antoine.

You cross a little stream.

A clearing in the forest.

And he shot himself right through the heart.
He knew exactly where his heart was at.
He didn't miss.

He fell backward on the ground. He was laid out on the ground.

Like Jesus on the cross,

with his arms spread out.

He died right away and right inside that stone circle
he had made with the pebbles from the stream.

> You could tell he didn't suffer.
> He looked so peaceful, like he felt good . . .
> like he . . . finally felt good.

And on his shirt he had pinned
a little piece of paper
and on it he had written:

> *Grace and Peace be with me.*

# Jo Carson

## I Cannot Remember All the Times . . .

I cannot remember all the times he hit me.
I might could count black eyes,
how many times I said I ran into doors
or fell down or stepped into the path
of any flying object except his fist.
Once I got a black eye playing softball.
The rest were him. Seven, eight.
I can name what of me he broke:
my nose, my arm, and four ribs
in the course of six years' marriage.
The ribs were after I said divorce
and in spite of a peace bond.
I spent the night in the hospital.
He did not even spend a night in jail.
The sheriff I helped elect does not
apply the law to family business.
He always swore he never meant to do it.
I do believe he never planned.
It was always just the day,
the way I looked at him afraid.
Maybe the first time he did not mean to do it,
maybe the broken ribs were for good luck.

I want to post this in ladies rooms,
write it on the tags of women's underwear,
write it on coupons to go in Tampax packages
because my ex-husband will want to marry again
and there is no tattoo where he can't see it
to tell the next woman who might fall in love with him.
After six months, maybe a year,
he will start with a slap you can brush off.
Leave when he slaps you.
When he begins to call you cunt and whore

and threatens to kill you if you try to go
it will almost be like teasing but it is not.
Keep two sets of car keys for yourself.
Take your children with you when you go.
If he is throwing things, he is drinking.
If he is drunk enough he cannot catch you.
A punch in the breast hurts worse than a punch in the jaw.
A hit with an object does more damage than a hit with a fist
unless he is so drunk he picks up a broom instead of a poker.
If you pick up the poker, he will try to get it.
If he gets it, he will hit you with it.
He probably will not kill you because you will pass out
and then, he is all the sudden sorry and he stops.
When he says he will not hit you again
as he drives you to the hospital,
both of you in tears and you in pain,
you have stayed much too long already.
Tell the people at the hospital the truth
no matter how much you think you love him.
Do not say you fell down stairs
no matter how much he swears he loves you.
He does love you, he loves you hurt
and he will hit you again.

## I Am Asking You to Come Back Home

I am asking you to come back home
before you lose your chance of seein' me alive.
You already missed your daddy.
You missed your Uncle Howard.
You missed Luciel. I kept them and I buried them.
You showed up for the funerals.
Funerals are the easy part.

You even missed that dog you left.
I dug him a hole and put him in it.

It was a Sunday morning but dead animals
don't wait no better than dead people.

My mama used to say she could feel herself
runnin' short of the breath of life. So can I.
And I am blessed tired of buryin' things I love.
Somebody else can do that job to me.
You'll be back here then, you come for funerals.

I'd rather you come back now and got my stories.
I've got whole lives of stories that belong to you.
I could fill you up with stories,
stories I ain't told nobody yet,
stories with your name, your blood in them.
Ain't nobody gonna hear them if you don't
and you ain't gonna hear them unless you get back home.

When I am dead, it will not matter
how hard you press your ear to the ground.


## The Day I Married . . .

The day I married, my mother
had one piece of wedding advice:
"Don't make good potato salad," she told me
"it's too hard to make
and you'll have to take something
every time you get invited somewhere.
Just cook up beans, people eat them too."

My mother was good at potato salad
and part of the memories of my childhood
have to do with endless batches made
for family get-togethers, church picnics,
Civitan suppers, Democratic party fund raisers,
whatever event called for potato salad.

I'd peel the hardboiled eggs.
My mother would pack her big red plastic picnic bowl
high with yellow potato salad (she used mustard)
and it would sit proud on endless tables
and come home empty.

What my mother might and could have said
is choose carefully what you get good at
cause you'll spend the rest of your life
doing it. But I didn't hear that.
I was young and anxious to please
and I knew her potato salad secrets.

And the thousand other duties
given to daughters by mothers
and sometimes I envy those women
who get by with pots of beans.

# Ana Castillo

## A Marriage of Mutes

In the house
that was his house
where the woman who lived there
cut the vegetables
hacked the chicken
boiled on the stove
and waited across the table
as he ate, with eyes that asked,
Was it all right? Was it enough?—
the woman who slept with him
changed the linen
scrubbed oil from his coveralls
hung laundry on the line
never sought the face of the woman
across the yard who hung sheets,
coveralls and underwear—
in the house where this man lived
so at peace with himself
the air grew sparse one morning.

The hall to the bathroom narrowed
as his feet grew angular and
head lightened.
He startled himself to hear his first
"caw!"—beating black wings against walls,
knocking down picture frames of the woman's
ancestors, the offspring's bronzed shoes
off the buffet.
One could only guess what he might
have said had his beak contained teeth.
The woman who always anticipated
his needs opened a window.
She would have wanted the crow to sit
on the couch

to read with her,
listen to music,
languish in a moment of peace
before the bird who was the man
she had lived with in such gratitude flew off,
but of course, it was too much to ask.

It had always been too much to ask.

# Lorna Dee Cervantes

## Freeway 280

Las casitas near the gray cannery,
nestled amid wild abrazos of climbing roses
and man-high red geraniums
are gone now. The freeway conceals it
all beneath a raised scar.

But under the fake windsounds of the open lanes,
in the abandoned lots below, new grasses sprout,
wild mustard remembers, old gardens
come back stronger than they were,
trees have been left standing in their yards.
Albaricoqueros, cerezos, nogales . . .
Viejitas come here with paper bags to gather greens.
Espinaca, verdolagas, yerbabuena . . .

I scramble over the wire fence
that would have kept me out.
Once, I wanted out, wanted the rigid lanes
to take me to a place without sun,
without the smell of tomatoes burning
on swing shift in the greasy summer air.

Maybe it's here
en los campos extraños de esta ciudad
where I'll find it, that part of me
mown under
like a corpse
or a loose seed.

## Uncle's First Rabbit

He was a good boy
making his way through
the Santa Barbara pines,
shifting the blast of fluff
as he leveled the rifle,
and the terrible singing began.
He was ten years old,
hunting my grandpa's supper.
He had dreamed of running,
shouldering the rifle to town,
selling it, and taking the next
train out.
       Fifty years
have passed and he still hears
that rabbit "just like a baby."
He remembers how the rabbit
stopped keening under the butt
of his rifle, how he brought
it home with tears streaming
down his blood-soaked jacket.
"That bastard. That bastard."
He cried all night and the week
after, remembering that voice
like his dead baby sister's,
remembering his father's drunken
kicking that had pushed her
into birth. She had a voice
like that, growing faint
at its end; his mother rocking,
softly, keening. He dreamed
of running, running
the bastard out of his life.
He would forget them, run down
the hill, leave his mother's
silent waters, and the sounds
of beating night after night.
       When war came,
he took the man's vow. He was
finally leaving and taking
the bastard's last bloodline

with him. At war's end, he could
still hear her, her soft
body stiffening under water
like a shark's. The color
of the water, darkening, soaking,
as he clung to what was left
of a ship's gun. Ten long hours
off the coast of Okinawa, he sang
so he wouldn't hear them.
He pounded their voices out
of his head, and awakened
to find himself slugging the bloodied
face of his wife.
    Fifty years
have passed and he has not run
the way he dreamed. The Paradise
pines shadow the bleak hills
to his home. His hunting hounds,
dead now. His father, long dead.
His wife, dying, hacking in the bed
she has not let him enter for the last
thirty years. He stands looking,
he mouths the words, "Die you bitch.
I'll live to watch you die." He turns,
entering their moss-soft livingroom.
He watches out the picture window
and remembers running: how he'll
take the new pickup to town, sell it,
and get the next train out.

## Beetles

A man who once loved me, told me
I knew nothing of beauty.
He had loved a double
more beautiful than I.

I'm hexed by a girl of pale heart,
a dove who wouldn't circle in day.
The thighs of her jeans are speckled with mustard.

Her hands are in her pockets too much of the time;
if they left, they would be birds, fragile, humming.
They are right where she puts them.
She's a farmer, plowing
the gray dirt.
She loves the land, its
ugliness.

I'm an ugly woman, weedlike,
elbowing my way through the perfect
grass. The best of what I am
is in the gravel behind the train yard
where obsidian chips lodge
in the rocks like beetles.
I burrow and glow.


## Lots: I


### The Alley

He told her
shut up and die.
The bed of shrubs
in the vacant lot
listened and filled
the fog with their
"Tsk, tsk."
She was so young,
only two years
more than a child.
She felt the flex
of his arm before
he touched her,
the wind of his fist
before he hit her.
But it was the glint
of steel at the throat
that cut through
to her voice.

She would not be
silent and still.
She would live,
arrogantly,
having wrestled
her death
and won.

## Lots: II

### Herself

I picked myself up        ignoring
whoever I was        slowly
noticing for the first time my body's stench
I made a list in my head
of all the names who could help me
and then        meticulously        I scratched
each one
        *they won't hear me burning*
        *inside of myself*
my used skin glistened
my first diamond

# Lillie D. Chaffin

## Escape

I walk treacherous mid-March
ice and snow to escape the hot dry walls,
grunting appreciation for the knife-sharp,
lung-drowning air.
                          The sounds
trigger a long buried scene:
Jane, a cousin far-removed, who went some
farther than her usual "little off"
one day waded into ice floating Johns Creek
chanting "Hallelujah! I freetize
the father, son and holly toast."
                                          Rising
from a shallow ditch, I say "Peace" to us.


## Dancing in the Dark

These stalls and squalls and sudden
temperature drops. I keep
turning corners and bumping
into feelings I thought
asleep, gone away or dead, feelings
that stop me with resemblance
to threadbare aprons, patchwork
quilts so new seamings are still puffed,
shoes that rub heels, pinch toes, graves
with stones leaning down a hill,
and faces that are beyond now:
enhanced by emotions, hidden
by their distance, I re-convince

myself that I am over
all this, past hurt and pain,
gone into a new country where
weathers are whatever tune I need
for dancing in this dark.

# Diana Chang

## "Energy Is Eternal Delight"

*(According to Han Suyin, a spark appears when the
acupuncture needle accurately contacts a point.)*

The patient, hanging fire,
   peels a tangerine

His equilibrium like August—
   a bright sleep he can't close his eyes on

The doctors needle emblems of time
   called nerves, a lung, despair

Almost knowing, he sheds his body
   in energy

He is only breath in any case,
   visionary

His biology dreamed out,
   sanity flaring

## On Gibson Lane, Sagaponack

It's not that I long for Chinese
       bodies

but I see a girl with blond hair
rocking by on a horse

and I realize
how foreign she is, too

light
and
strange

riding along the same edge

# Sandra Cisneros

## The So-and-So's

Your other women are well-behaved.
Your Magnolias and Simones.
Those with the fine brave skin like moon
and limbs of violin and bones like roses.
They bloom nocturnal and are done
with nary a clue behind them.
Nary a clue. Save one or two.

Here is the evidence of them.
Occasionally the plum print
of a mouth on porcelain.
And here the strands of mermaids
discovered on the bathtub shores.
And now and again, tangled in
the linen—love's smell—
musky, unmistakable,
terrible as tin.

But love is nouveau.
Love is liberal as a general
and allows. Love with no say so
in these matters, no X nor claim nor title,
shuts one wicked eye and courteously
abides.

I cannot out
with such civility.
I don't know how to
go—not mute as snow—
without my dust and clatter.
I am no so-and-so.

I who arrived deliberate as Tuesday
without my hat and shoes

with one rude black tattoo
and purpose thick as pumpkin.

One day I'll dangle
from your neck, public as a jewel.
One day I'll write my name on everything
as certain as a trail of bread.
I'll leave my scent of smoke.
I'll paint my wrists.
You'll see. You'll see.
I will not out so easily.

I was here. As loud as trumpet.
As real as pebble in the shoe.
A tiger tooth. A definite voodoo.
Do not erase me.

Let me bequeath
a single pomegranate seed,
a tell-tale clue.
I want to be like you. A who.

And let them bleed.


## My Wicked Wicked Ways

This is my father.
See? He is young.
He looks like Errol Flynn.
He is wearing a hat
that tips over one eye,
a suit that fits him good,
and baggy pants.
He is also wearing
those awful shoes,
the two-toned ones
my mother hates.

Here is my mother.
She is not crying.
She cannot look into the lens
because the sun is bright.
The woman,
the one my father knows,
is not here.
She does not come till later.

My mother will get very mad.
Her face will turn red
and she will throw one shoe.
My father will say nothing.
After a while everyone
will forget it.
Years and years will pass.
My mother will stop mentioning it.

This is me she is carrying.
I am a baby.
She does not know
I will turn out bad.


## His Story

I was born under a crooked star.
So says my father.
And this perhaps explains his sorrow.

An only daughter
whom no one came for
and no one chased away.

It is an ancient fate.
A family trait we trace back
to a great aunt no one mentions.

Her sin was beauty.
She lived mistress.
Died solitary.

There is as well
the cousin with the famous
how shall I put it?
profession.

She ran off with the colonel.
And soon after,
the army payroll.

And, of course,
grandmother's mother
who died a death of voodoo.
There are others.

For instance,
my father explains,
in the Mexican papers
a girl with both my names
was arrested for audacious crimes
that began by disobeying fathers.

Also, and here he pauses,
the Cubano who sells him shoes
says he too knew a Sandra Cisneros
who was three times cursed a widow.

You see.
An unlucky fate is mine
to be born woman in a family of men.

Six sons, my father groans,
all home.
And one female,
gone.

## 14 de julio

Today, *catorce de julio,*
a man kissed a woman in the rain.
On the corner of Independencia y Cinco de Mayo.
A man kissed a woman.

Because it is Friday.
Because no one has to go to work tomorrow.
Because, in direct opposition to Church and State,
a man kissed a woman
oblivious to the consequence of sorrow.

A man kisses a woman unashamed,
within a universe of two I'm certain.
Beside the sea of taxicabs on Cinco de Mayo.
In front of an open-air statue.
On an intersection busy with tourists and children.
Every day little miracles like this occur.

A man kisses a woman in the rain
and I am envious of that simple affirmation.
I who timidly took and timidly gave—
you who never admitted a public grace.
We of the half-dark who were unbrave.

# Cheryl Clarke

## Of Flaxie and Althea

In 1943 Althea was a welder
very dark
very butch
and very proud
loved to cook, sew, and drive a car
and did not care who knew
she kept company with a woman
who met her everyday after work
in a tight dress and high heels
light-skinned and high-cheekboned
who loved to shoot, fish, play poker
and did not give a damn
who knew her "man" was a woman.

Althea was gay and strong in 1945
and could sing a good song
from underneath her welder's mask
and did not care who heard her sing
her song to a woman.

Flaxie was careful and faithful
mindful of her Southern upbringing
watchful of her tutored grace
long as they treated her like a lady
she did not give a damn
who called her a "bulldagger."

In 1950 Althea wore suits and ties.
Flaxie's favorite colors were pink and blue.
People openly challenged their flamboyance
but neither cared a fig
who thought them "queer" or "funny."

When the girls bragged over break
of their sundry loves,

Flaxie blithely told them
her old lady Althea took her dancing
every weekend
and did not give a damn
who knew she clung to a woman.

When the boys on her shift
complained of their wives,
Althea boasted
of how smart her "stuff" Flaxie was
and did not care
who knew she loved the mind of a woman.

In 1955 when Flaxie got pregnant
and Althea lost her job
Flaxie got herself on relief
and did not care how many caseworkers
threatened midnite raids.

Althea was set up and went to jail
for writing numbers in 1958.
Flaxie visited her every week with gifts
and hungered openly for her thru the bars
and did not give a damn
who knew she waited for a woman.

When her mother died in 1965 in New Orleans
Flaxie demanded that Althea walk beside her
in the funeral procession
and did not care how many aunts and uncles
knew she slept with a woman.

When she died in 1970
Flaxie fought Althea's proper family
not to have her laid out in lace
and dressed the body herself
and did not care who knew
she'd made her way with a woman.

# Jan Clausen

## Sestina, Winchell's Donut House

Watching the black hours through to morning
I'd set out each successive tray of grease-
cooked donuts on the rack, chocolate and pink-
frosted, to harden beneath the fluorescent light,
talk to crazy Harry, count the change,
listen to top-forty radio. Mostly, I was alone.

Every stranger's suspect when you're alone.
A woman was beaten badly early one morning
by a man who sneaked in the back while she made change,
so I'd rehearse scenarios of scooping grease,
flinging it at the assailant's face, cooking the light
or dark flesh to curl away at the impact, angry pink.

The cab drivers came in every night, faces polished pink
and boyish, arriving in pairs or alone.
Their cabs clotted like moths at the building's light.
They were outlaws and brothers, despised men who rise
                    in the morning.
They'd swagger, still dapper, if fattened on sweets and grease,
call me sugar and honey. I smiled. I kept the change.

Often I was too busy to see the darkness change,
flush from black to blue to early pink.
At four o'clock, my face smeared with congealed grease,
I think I was happiest, although most alone.
The harder hours were those of fullblown morning,
fighting depression, sleeping alone in the light.

Linda came in at six, awash with light,
businesslike, making sure there'd be enough change
to get her through the rigors of the morning.
She had a hundred uniforms; I remember pink.

73

Sometimes she'd cheat, leave me to work alone,
sneak out to flirt in parked cars, fleeing lifetimes
                  of grease.

I can see her cranking the hopper, measuring grease,
indefatigable, wired on coffee, just stopping to light
her cigarettes. She didn't want to be alone.
It was only my fantasy that she could change,
stop wearing that silly, becoming pink,
burn free of the accidents, husband and children,
                  some morning.

I remember walking home those mornings, smelling of grease,
amazed in summer's most delicate pink early light,
to shower, change, and sleep out the hot day alone.


## No Hay Fronteras

      Just that way I wanted to touch you
    the way death and life
        are lovers
I'm not talking about the horrors
      this is also a city of peace
          though the kids lie buried
    in yards
on the blocks
    where they fell
      in hardpacked dirt
    near their mothers' cookstoves
      and washtubs
    and on every wall is tallied
the price of a ragged freedom
         and we shout ¡no pasarán!
    and worry about November

Pequeña ciudad loca
    hanging tough

with a hole in the heart
                whose grumbling cabbies
        calculate destinations
    by ghost-memory of buildings
                twelve years vanished in the earthquake
Goats quartered in the rubble
    turkeys venerable in doorways
            and platoons of roosters
        dueling in the dawn
            Sad, scrappy negrito boys
        hawking *Barricada*
and Soviet tourists
            in white straw cowboy hats
and tall laughing painters
    who had to leave Salvador
        Market women
    in their eternal ruffled aprons
        Sandino's daughters
            butch in khaki

        No boundaries, I thought
        an open city
    and lost myself a little
                unsure
        how to read the season
a hundred brooms endlessly sweeping
            sweeping in circles
                the endlessly falling
        banana-colored leaves

I wanted to tell you: a country without winter

        But I'll never learn to predict
            the syncopations
        of tropical rain
            beating against this heat
        in the dark

a green
   primeval desolation

It could go either way, I thought
   La puerta
     está abierta
        You could walk from Managua
     to Nueva York

*July, 1984*

## Being Aware

Men are drawn to my ass by
my death-trance blue eyes
and black hair, tiny outfit,
while my father is home with
a girl, moved by things
I could never think clearly.

Men smudge me onto a bed,
drug me stupid, gossip and
photograph me till I'm famous
in alleys, like one of those
jerk offs who stare from
the porno I sort of admire.

I'm fifteen. Screwing means
more to the men than to me.
I daydream right through it
while money puts chills on
my arms, from this to that
grip. I was meant to be naked.

Hey, Dad, it's been like this
for decades. I was always
approached by your type, given
dollars for hours. I took a
deep breath, stripped and they
never forgot how I trembled.

It means tons to me. Aside
from the obvious heaven
when cumming, there's times
I'm with them that I'm happy

at the other guy
, which is progress.

Or, nights when I'm angry,
if in a man's arms moving
slowly to the quietest music—
his hands on my arms, in my
hands, in the small of my back
take me back before everything.

## Hustlers

Two beers screw my head up.
I lean back against a dark wall.
My long hair drifts in my eyes.
Let's say the moon makes a decision.
I land the corner legend surrounds.
I say more than I pretend to.
I prefer to be fucked to The Beatles.
I stand with the guys I resemble.
Jerry, Tom, Dick, Sam, Julian, Max, Timmy.
Guess which of those names is perfect.
We dream of a casual million.
We light our cigarettes gently.
I take what the night has to offer.
I roll a ripe peach from one wrist to the other.
I can't speak I'm so fucking stupid.
Our bodies are simply stupendous.
When we breathe, it takes us apart.
You know. You're inside us.

## John Kennedy Jr. at Twenty-One

John, his mother and sister step from
the black limousine. They're lit brighter
than everyone else by a round of flashes
and glare off the mini-cam kliegs. He

bites his lip. "This again." Friends
of the family clear a path to the grave.
Once they've knelt, the crowd of re-
porters shouts some condolences. John
thinks they're lying, even the veterans
he remembers from Washington. He grips
his mother's arm. "Mom," he whispers,
"let's make this brief." She nods and
on that motion's down swing her neck
crumples up. The cameras click. She's
fifty-one. Her cross, breathy mouth
says, "Yes," with the s held forever it
seems. She's annoyed. Caroline stares
straight ahead, swearing out of one
side of her mouth. Later in A.P. wire
photos she'll seem stoned out and the
rumors will start. But here lies one
shimmering nameplate piled with their
world's paltry backyard of flora. John
looks at the flowers, his knees, his
nails. He listens to what the report-
ers are babbling. He lowers his head.
The platform's imperiously gray, just
the way the storm left it. His knees
are soaked through with water. His
eyes are left cold by the long walk
from him to their reason for being
blue. When he returns to his feet at
his mother's command and starts back
to the car his head's ducked. One
hand's drawn in front of his face so
the cameras can't pick his thoughts.
They're impenetrable but they will
not be glossed over, unlike the grass.

# Sam Cornish

## Harriet in the Promised Land

*From the book by Jacob Lawrence*

in a red dress
a woman on her knees
washes the floor
a hundred years ago

she is shaping the life of her children
she thinks as a woman
does of freedom
a dark place in the woods
where the north enters the trees

she wonders if words mean history        a woman
losing her children
if reading is a crime
she does not ask for pity

there is a damp rag on the floor
she wipes
in the dress she slept in        the dress
she had her children in

she scrubs the floor
does not brush her teeth
she picks them with straw or sticks

she moves on her knees
and watches the ceiling in the water
reflected in the water

everything in her life
is hard like the floor she
touches

the water in her hands
the water is between her legs
her body like a sack of muscle
her hands are dark with water

she wonders about her children
how many children      if she could count
pass her fingers
about her body
the words she would find if she could read

she gathers water
like sounds in her head
she kneels like a slave
in church
like a slave preparing to dance
in front of the big house
she pretends to be quiet
her mind is grinding
glass
pissing in the evening meal

## Women Walk

women walk because
    airplanes
    drop engines
    into playgrounds
    sea gulls
    fly unto air
    conditioners
    meat in cans
    destroys the mind
women walk because men with draft
    cards are tired
    of Canada and find
    prison uncomfortable

women walk because death can
    be a guest at the dinner
    table and clean his plate
women walk because they
    know words are never
    enough when you want to be touched.


## Fannie Lou Hamer

fannie
lou
hamer
never
heard
of
in chicago
was known for
her
big
black
mouth
in the south
fannie lou
ate
her greens
watched
her land
and wanted
to
vote

men went
to the bottom
of the river
for wanting less
but fannie

got up
went to the courthouse

big as a fist
black as the ground
underfoot

# Jayne Cortez

## I See Chano Pozo

A very fine conga of sweat
a very fine stomp of the right foot
a very fine platform of sticks
a very fine tube of frictional groans
a very fine can of belligerent growls
a very fine hoop of cubano yells
very fine      very fine

Is there anyone finer today      olé      okay
Oye      I say
I see Chano Pozo
Chano Pozo from Havana Cuba
                                        You're the one
You're the one who made Atamo into
a tattooed motivator of revolutionary spirits

You're the one who made Mpebi into
an activated slasher of lies

You're the one who made Donno into
an armpit of inflammable explosives

You're the one who made Obonu into
a circle of signifying snakes

You're the one who made Atumpan's head strike
against
the head of a bird    everynight    everyday
in your crisscrossing chant
in your cross river mouth
                                        You're the one

Oye      I say
Chano
what made you roar like a big brazos flood
what made you yodel like a migrating frog
what made you shake like atomic heat
what made you jell into a ritual pose
Chano      Chano      Chano
what made your technology of thumps so new so
mean
I say
is there anyone meaner than Chano Pozo
                              from Havana Cuba

Oye
I'm in the presence of ancestor
                         Chano Pozo

Chano connector of two worlds
You go and celebrate again with
the compañeros in Santiago
   and tell us about it
You go to the spirit house of Antonio Maceo
and tell us about it
You go to Angola
and tell us about it
You go to Calabar
and tell us about it
You go see the slave castles
you go see the massacres
you go see the afflictions
you go see the battlefields
you go see the warriors
you go as a healer
you go conjurate
you go mediate
you go to the cemetery of drums
return and tell us about it

85

Lucumí      Abakẃa  Lucumí     Abakẃa

Olé      okay
Is there anyone finer today
Oye      I say

did you hear
Mpintintoa smoking in the palm of his hands
did you hear
Ilya Ilu booming through the cup of his clap
did you hear
Ntenga sanding on the rim of his rasp
did you hear
Siky Akkua stuttering like a goat sucking hawk
did you hear
Bata crying in a nago tongue
did you hear
Fontomfrom speaking through the skull of a dog
did you hear it     did you hear it     did you hear it

A very fine tree stump of drones
a very fine shuffle of shrines
a very fine turn of the head
a very fine tissue of skin
a very fine smack of the lips
a very fine pulse
a very fine encuentro
very fine     very fine     very fine
Is there anyone finer than

Chano Pozo from Havana Cuba
Oye      I say
I see Chano Pozo

# Melvin Dixon

## Tour Guide: *La Maison des Esclaves*

*Ile de Gorée, Senegal*

He speaks of voyages:
men traveling spoon-fashion,
women dying in afterbirth,
babies clinging
to salt-dried nipples.
For what his old eyes still see
his lips have few words. Where
his flat thick feet still walk
his hands crack
into a hundred lifelines.

Here waves rush to shore
breaking news that we return
to empty rooms
where the sea is nothing calm.
And sun, tasting the skin
of black men,
leaves teeth marks.

The rooms are empty until he speaks.
His guttural French is a hawking trader.
His quick Wolof a restless warrior.
His slow, impeccable syllables
a gentleman trader. He tells
in their own language
what they have done.

Our touring maps and cameras ready
we stand in the weighing room
where chained men paraded firm backs,
their women open, full breasts,

and children,
rows of shiny teeth.

Others watched from the balcony,
set the price in guilders, francs,
pesetas and English pounds. Later
when he has finished we too
can leave our coins
where stiff legs dragged
in endless bargain.

He shows how some sat knee-bent
in the first room.
Young virgins waited in the second.
In the third, already red,
the sick and dying
gathered near the exit to the sea.

In the weighing room again
he takes a chain to show us
how it's done. We take
photographs to remember,
others leave coins to forget.
No one speaks
except iron on stone
and the sea
where nothing's safe.

He smiles for he has spoken
of the ancestors: his, ours.
We leave quietly, each alone,
knowing that they who come after us
and breaking
in these tides will find
red empty rooms
to measure long journeys.

# Sharon Doubiago

## Appalachian Song

I see a dirt road inside myself and on it I am walking.
At the far end where the sun is setting
are my children, all the western scattering
of my flesh.

Here are the voices I hear, the unaccountable melancholy,
the dark hearts of my grandparents, storied in my flesh.
When I look to the hills I hear
shattering like glass, the red in the loam
soaked from me.

Near the cabin at the clearing's center
I hear a mournful Scottish melody.
When I walk amidst flowering dogwood
a thousand tongues lift their words to me.

*Call my name in the act of love.* I am full of loss
and the shadowy Cherokee. At night I fall
into our migrations, settlers drifting across
the Great Barrier.

The cold winters you say, the loss of war paint,
the images tattooed on the skin of my brain.
My daughter in the river we drink, its body
lifting her before she knew the body of a man.

When you call me, your face, bald as the eroded hills,
is blessedly here, between me and these scenes.
But when we ride the boy in your scrotum, which stores,
like glass, the ruins of this place, you pull
houses full of blood, mountains full of smoke, down
on top of me.

## Signal Hill

My father leaves us in the car
and drinks beer in the Hilltop Bar.
The red neon woman who wears only
a ruffled apron and high heels
carries a tray of drinks
around and around the top of the hill
to the giant robots that pump
the fields.

In her red light my baby
brother and sister in the backseat of the car
are contorted in screams Daddy doesn't hear
over the jukebox and high squeals
of the bar maid I never see and wonder
if she too wears no clothes.
I hear her cry *ah Babes!*
We come here every Friday when he gets paid
but my brother and sister are still afraid
of the nodding creatures in the dark
we are parked between.

The city spreads beneath us
in a rainbow-spilled oil puddle.
The harbor is lit with battleships
that strain at their ropes
toward bigger war across the sea.

The dirty men keep driving up beside us.
I sit in the mother's seat
and they say to me things men say
to mothers.

I study her gay nipples
and wonder if mine will get that way.
Far below, on the shore of the Pike
a man sits on top of the neon needle
for months just to break a record.
One man says of him as he runs
his middle finger across the dewy window

of my face,
*Tough, not gettin any.*

When Daddy comes home through the door
beneath the spinning neon lady
it is the only time I ever see him
happy. Now we drive the cold side
of Signal Hill, the backside of the city and sea
so dark even now in the middle of the twentieth century
they hide the dying, the ones
they still can't cure, my mother
in her sanitarium.

We drive across the starry oil field
to her window where she lies
in the contagion ward we kids cannot go near.
My father taps on her dark window
and soon my mother lifts the pane
and puts her porcelain hand
out into the dark for him.

He puts one of his
on one of her large breasts
that are not like the red neon woman's
and sometimes lays his head
on her white arm that knows no sun
and between the groans of the field
letting go its oil
I hear him sigh
*oh, honey,* and sometimes
*jesus*

# James A. Emanuel

## Deadly James (For All the Victims of Police Brutality)

The killer-cops, the San Diego three,
what made them think you deadly, James?

I take their guilty heads into my arms;
I cradle them,
my tendons hush their eyes,
illumine them to see the years roll back:
your little window, James, unsealed,
your palomino rocking horse,
his glassy eyes unquiet
when the sudden blood that splashed his ivory mane
told you the table knife you sucked on
was different, could also spit upon the tawny rug
breathtaking tracks—
deadly, James.

I embrace their heads more tightly;
their veins bulge to understand you, James,
you, hardly old enough to run,
dancing solitary in the Brooklyn rain
your older playmates dashed from,
your arms and lips and laughter reaching up
for all the sky could pour
upon the rivers capering inside you—
deadly rivers, James?

I hug their heads
with strength I had saved for you, James;
their eyeballs darken as they strain with me
to find you practicing your saxophone,
lying in the quilted heaps your bed poked up
around your stocking feet—the littered outpost
of that farther wilderness you made your room,
"NO ENTRY" blazed across the door

to guard your heartbeats
when your golden horn *believed* its one-man note—
that wild, sweet loneliness you cried—
beguiling neighbors into forgiveness
before you fumbled scales beginners know.
You       began at the top, James,
deadly.

I clasp their heads more fiercely,
empowered by the memory of you
stranded where they bled you down
into your smallest drop,
gunhammers cocked and nightsticks sinewed—
all three bewildered to find beauty
defiantly beyond them,
a tiny, dark-brown flower: the grain of you, James,
erect,
watered back to momentary life
by your manful tears.

In my iron arms their heads turn dry,
drop hollow to the ground . . .
If your new unearthly wisdom bids you,
raise them.
But whenever you feel blood again,
or rain, or music,
pray your innocence be deadlier, James,
   much
      deadlier.

# Lynn Emanuel

## The Photograph of Ramona Posing While Father Sketches Her in Charcoal

Father is transforming Ramona
Into a streamline of flesh
Smudging the nipple with his thumb
In the tough, awkward way
Children rub their eyes when tired.
The sea is smooth as oiled stone again
Between Cagnes-sur-Mer and Cap Bénat
And the shadows full of models' empty shoes
Because this is 1938 and the tedium and heat
Of the Côte d'Azure.
Even Ramona is boring in the slick
Cool silver of her flesh.
Life is not pretty
Although she does not believe it.
This girl whose gold tooth
Father polished with his tongue
Could make anyone forget the wild buttocks of Rubens
And fill the fields with weeping painters
For whom the world has become a studio
Of beautiful forgeries.
Life is not pretty
Although they do not know it yet—
And in that heat
And the streets full of Germans.

## Frying Trout While Drunk

Mother is drinking to forget a man
Who could fill the woods with invitations:
Come with me he whispered and she went
In his Nash Rambler, its dash

Where her knees turned green
In the radium dials of the '50s.
When I drink it is always 1953,
Bacon wilting in the pan on Cook Street
And mother, wrist deep in red water,
Laying a trail from the sink
To a glass of gin and back.
She is a beautiful, unlucky woman
In love with a man of lechery so solid
You could build a table on it
And when you did the blues would come to visit.
I remember all of us awkwardly at dinner,
The dark slung across the porch,
And then mother's dress falling to the floor,
Buttons ticking like seeds spit on a plate.
When I drink I am too much like her—
The knife in one hand and in the other
The trout with a belly white as my wrist.
I have loved you all my life
She told him and it was true
In the same way that all her life
She drank, dedicated to the act itself,
She stood at this stove
And with the care of the very drunk
Handed him the plate.


## For Me at Sunday Sermons, the Serpent

coming lightly, perfectly
   into the garden
      was as smart as Eve was

pink, fat & pliant
   was tough as a root,
      but blue

or green:
   a reed, a stem;
      the uninterruptedness of him

from tail to lip, all
   one thing, consistent
      as a walking stick.

Or he was a ruby
   cummerbund, a glove
      on its way to the opera

dropped
   in the dust
      of this god forsaken town.

Beside his motionless chill
   Ely, Nevada
      was as dull as two buttons.

He was the green
   light, the go-ahead,
      the spark, the road,

the ticket out.


## The Technology of Inspiration

I am tired of the tundra of the mind,
where a few shabby thoughts hunker
around a shabby fire. All day from my window
I watch girls and boys hanging out
in the dark arcades of adolescent desire.

Tonight, everything is strict with cold,
the houses closed, the ice botched by skaters.
I am tired of saying things about the world,
and yet, sometimes, these streets are so
slick and bold they remind me of the wet

zinc bar at the Café Marseilles, and suddenly the sea
is green and lust is everywhere in a red cravate,
leaning on his walking stick and whispering,

*I am a city, you are my pilgrim,*
*meet me this evening, Love, Pierre.*

And so I have to get up and walk downstairs
just to make sure the city's still secure
in its leafless and wintery slime
and it still is and yet somewhere on that
limitless, starlit sea-coast of my past,

Pierre's red tie burns like a small fire.
And all at once my heart stumbles like a
drunken sailor, and I, an ordinary woman,
am adrift in the *bel aujourd'hui* of Pittsburgh.

# Martín Espada

## The Spanish of Our Out-Loud Dreams

*para Nora Elena Díaz*

You took your father
from the Bronx hospital
where the radiation failed,
to an island hospital
surrounded by palm trees
and hallways of nurses
who understood the Spanish
of his out-loud dreams.
Their hands gestured
at the hopeless chart.

Los puertorriqueños are always looking
for a place to sleep:
not in the houses we scrape clean for others,
not in the migrant camps we leave
after the crop is busheled,
not on the buses blowing out their bad lungs
in the horseshoe curve of highways,
or on the beaches of an island
spiked with the picket fence of tall hotels.

Back in the Bronx
and you're packing again,
moving southwest.
Last night you cried,
your black eyes shimmering darker
than the room
where we tried to sleep,
crying like your father cried
when you pulled away
from the hospital bed,
and for all the nights

we have wandered with stuffed bags,
not staying long enough
to learn the language.
My hand slipped through the night-thicket
of your hair,
as if the circling of my fingers
could give you rest.

In Puerto Rico,
your father tries to still
the jumping memory
of a numbers runner,
trying to sleep
between hospital-white curtains.

Let him sleep
where I slept:
shining in your passionate blackness,
the vigil of your shimmering gaze.


## Manuel Is Quiet Sometimes

He was quiet again,
driving east on 113,
near the slaughterhouse
on the day after Christmas,
not mourning,
but almost bowed,
like it is after the funeral
of a distant relative,
thoughtful,
sorrow on the border at dusk.

Vietnam was a secret.
Some men there collected ears,
some gold teeth.
Manuel collected the moist silences

between bursts of mortar.
He would not tell
what creatures laughed in his sleep,
or what blood was still drying
from bright to dark
in moments of boredom
and waiting.
A few people knew
about the wound,
a jabbing in his leg
(though he refused
to limp);
I knew about the time
he went AWOL.

Driving east on 113,
he talked
about how he keeps
the car running
in winter. It's
a good car,
he said.
There was the brief illumination
of passing headlights,
and slaughterhouse smoke
halted in the sky.

Another night,
the night of the Chicano dance,
Manuel's head swung slow and lazy
with drinking.
He smiled repeatedly,
a polite amnesiac,
and drank other people's beer,
waiting for the dancers
to leave their tables
so he could steal the residue
in plastic cups.

It was almost 2 AM
when he toppled,

aimless as something beheaded,
collapsing so he huddled
a prisoner on the floor.

The shell of his body
swung elbows
when we pulled him up.
He saw me first,
seeing a stranger.
His eyes were the color
of etherized dreams,
eyes that could
castrate the enemy,
easy murder watching me
with no reflection.

This is what he said:
"I never lied
to you, man."


## Tiburón

East 116th
and a long red car
stalled with the hood up
roaring salsa
like a prize shark
mouth yanked open
and down into the stomach
the radio
of the last fisherman
still tuned
to his lucky station

# Where the Disappeared Would Dance

*Ponce, Puerto Rico 1985*

The shoeshine man squats at the hotel door,
points and shouts at the walkers
scraping his pavement,
under cheap loudspeakers
distorting "¡baratiiisimo!"
from the discount store;
under the busy hands of the jobless,
jabbing with streetcorner talk.

Ponce: the plaza crooked with detours
and stopped construction,
cars hot and snorting with impatience.
Above the bright rough signs
that trade in dollars,
balconies are crust-fragile, shutters nailed,
and windows keep the stunned faces
that remember Spain.
Even the festivals now
wear factory-masks,
and anglo-american soldiers
stride through the parade crowd.

The labors of cement in Ponce
paid for a banker's art museum
and centuries of European painting.
No one from the plaza goes there,
but a man thin as disease,
in pava straw hat and a white suit
left by the dead to charity,
brags to the sandwich stand
that he knows the governor.

Away from the factory road,
aboriginal stones circle a field
where the disappeared would dance,
where god-carvings still listen
for songs of worship,

and wild grass thickens
over the skeletons of caciques.

A shallow blue light
drifts between mountains
with a minute rain,
and the leaves of moriviví
are closing.

# Mari Evans

## A Man Without Food

Then the leader of the people
stubborn and stony
faced the cameras

He had swallowed his spittle
and could not wet his lips
"A man without food" he said
his lips parched and cracked
"is an animal"
"A man without food is an animal"
he said, confronting the cameras
His lips dry against his teeth

## Limited Aggression

O there are lands
    and in them
one-armed children watch
        horror-stilled
eyes lasered past any
acknowledgement
    motionless     they
are not moved by     wind
Wind seamed with death
caterwauling a wild anguish

Violated widows twist
soil ragged hems

their bony fingers
a forgetfulness

They will stare forever
down the dusty
                    vacant
                        road

# Edward Field

## The Tailspin

Going into a tailspin
in those days meant curtains.
No matter how hard you pulled back on the stick
the nose of the plane wouldn't come up.

Spinning round, headed for a target of earth,
the whine of death in the wing struts,
instinct made you try to pull out of it that way, by force,
and for years aviators spiraled down and crashed.

Who could have dreamed that the solution
to this dreaded aeronautical problem
was so simple?
Every student flier learns this nowadays:
You move the joystick in the direction of the spin
and like a miracle the plane stops turning
and you are in control again
to pull the nose up out of the dive.

In panic we want to push the stick away from the spin,
wrestle the plane out of it,
but the trick is, as in everything,
to go with the turning willingly,
rather than fight, give in, go with it,
and that way come out of your tailspin whole.

# Robert Glück

## The Chronicle

### 1

A swank luncheon thrown in Union Square by San Francisco
society's premiere hostess broke up today with apple cores
& curses & police drawing guns.

### 2

It was a catered affair featuring white gloved waiters,
staged by Charlotte Mailliard (pronounced Ma-yard) in
honor of I. Magnin exec. John Brunelle. A section of the
square was cordoned off & decorated with pastel balloons.

### 3

A bar was set up & drinks began pouring by noon. These
events excited considerable interest in onlookers, which
deepened as 40 guests sat down to spoon up their
vichyssoise, wash it down with chilled Pinot Blanc &
proceed to their avocados stuffed with shrimp.

### 4

90 minutes: murmurings turned to jeers: Rich Pigs Go
Home. Psychiatrist Richard Kunin, laying his napkin
down, rose to his feet & sought to reason.

### 5

"I told them, 'It can be painful being on the outside
looking in.' I said, 'I've been there before and I
suppose I will again.' " And by extension will they dine

one day at the table of Charlotte Mailliard? In this
way he bribed them with the distant mansions of country-
western music.


## Personal Reflection

Dr. Kunin functions as the mediating idealogue. He
belongs to the echelon that works for its betters by
creating imaginary resolutions of real contradictions.
(For ex., Charlotte Mailliard remained blandly intact,
said "They were the entertainment.")


## 6

Jeers resumed & drowned out the music. The guests
uneasily swallowed their long-stemmed strawberries.
"We didn't want to lose face in front of the enemy."


## 7

When patrolmen Walsh & Scott arrived the first apple
cores were flying and the air was blue and red with curses
and rhetoric. They pulled their guns and shouldered their
way, politely saying "Excuse me, excuse me."


## 8

By this time the waiters were assembling the silver in
some haste. Charlotte Mailliard, who this week gave
a party for dogs, said Brunelle always wanted to eat lunch
there & never got the chance.


## Personal Reflection

More interesting than her character is the question: what
forces generate interior landscapes of blackmail & cocktail
parties for dogs? When asked her view by the press the
rich rich rich Charlotte Mailliard answered: I give more
than I've received.

9

Three men were arrested. Two escaped. Nabbed: Richard Sawyer, 26, unemployed truck driver from Susanville. He called the *Chronicle* from City Prison: "I was just walking through the park & saw all the people & the balloons & the police grabbed hold of me."

# Gogisgi/Carroll Arnett

## The Old Man Said: One

Some will tell
you it doesn't
matter. That is
a lie. Everything,
every single thing
matters. And
nothing good
happens fast.

## Early Song

As the sun rises
high enough to
warm the frost
off the pine needles,

I rise to make
four prayers of
thanksgiving for
this fine clear day,

for this good brown
earth, for all
brothers and sisters,
for the dark blood

that runs through me
in a great circle
back into this
good brown earth.

## Song of the Breed

Don't offend
the fullbloods,
don't offend
the whites,
stand there in
the middle
of the god-
damned road
and get hit.

## Death Song

I am here only
a little while
I have loved
the joy of the earth
hello death

*Ayohu Kanogisdi*

*aya ahaniquo*
*usdi nahiyu*
*ayagvgeyu*
*ulihelisdi elohi*
*osiyo ayohu*

# Jessica Hagedorn

## The Song of Bullets

Formalized
by middle age
we avoid crowds
but still
love music.

Day after day
with less surprise
we sit
in apartments
and count
the dead.

Awake,
my daughter croons
her sudden cries
and growls
my new language.
While she sleeps
we memorize
a list of casualties:

The photographer's brother
the doctor is missing.
Or I could say:
"Victor's brother Oscar
has been gone for two years . . .
It's easier for the family
to think of him dead."

Victor sends
a Christmas card

from El Salvador:
"Things still the same."

And there are others
who don't play
by the rules—
someone else's brother
perhaps mine
languishes in a hospital;
everyone's grown tired
of his nightmares
and pretends
he's not there.

Someone else's father
perhaps mine
will be executed
when the time comes.
Someone else's mother
perhaps mine
telephones incessantly
her husband is absent
her son has gone mad
her lover has committed suicide
she's a survivor
who can't appreciate
herself.

The sight
of my daughter's
pink and luscious flesh
undoes me.
I fight
my weakening rage
I must remember
to commit
those names to memory
and stay angry.

Friends send postcards:
"Alternating between hectic

*social* Manila life & rural wonders
of Sagata . . . on to Hongkong and Bangkok—
Love . . ."

Assassins cruise the streets
in obtrusive limousines
sunbathers idle
on the beach

War is predicted
in five years
ten years
any day now
I always thought
it was already happening

snipers and poets locked
in a secret embrace
the country
my child may never see

a heritage
of women in heat
and men
skilled at betrayal

dancing
to the song
of bullets.

# Joy Harjo

## Grace

*For Jim Welch, and of course, Wind*

I think of Wind and her wild ways the year we had nothing to lose
and lost it anyway in the cursed country of the Fox. We still talk
about that winter, how the cold froze imaginary buffalo on the stuffed
horizon of snowbanks. The haunting voices of the starved and mutilated
broke fences, crashed our thermostat dreams, and we couldn't stand it
one more time. So once again we lost a winter in stubborn memory, walked
through cheap apartment walls, skated through fields of ghosts into
a town that never wanted us, in the epic search for grace.

Like Coyote, like Rabbit we could not contain our terror and clowned
our way through a season of false midnights. We had to swallow
that town with laughter, so it would go down easy as honey. And one
morning as the sun struggled to break ice, and our dreams had found
us with coffee and pancakes in a truckstop along highway eighty; we
found grace.

I could say grace was a woman with time on her hands, or a white
buffalo escaped from memory. But in that dingy light it was a promise
of balance. We once again understood the talk of animals, and spring
was lean and hungry with the hope of children and corn.

I would like to say, with grace, we picked ourselves up and walked
into the spring thaw. We didn't; the next season was worse. You went
home to Leech Lake to work with the tribe and I went South. And Wind,
I am still crazy. I know there is something larger than the memory of a
dispossessed people. We have seen it.

## Healing Animal

On this day when you have needed to sleep forever,
to forgive the pained animal kneading
                                        your throat.
*Sleep*, your back curled against my belly.
I will make you something to drink,
                                        from a cup of frothy stars
from the *somewhere there is the perfect sound*
*called up from the best told stories*
                                        *of benevolent gods,*
*who have nothing better to do.*
                                And I ask you,
*what bitter words are ruining your soft skinned village,*
because I want to make a poem that will cup
                        the inside of your throat
like the fire in the palm of a healing animal. Like,
the way Coltrane knew love in the fluid shape
of a saxophone
                that could change into the wings of a blue angel.
He tasted the bittersweet roots of this crazy world,
and spit it out into the center of our musical
                                        jazzed globe.
Josiah's uncle brought his music
            to the Papago center of the world
                        and music climbed out of his trombone
into the collected heartbeat of his tribe.
They had never heard anything like it,
                but it was the way they had remembered, the way
"Chief" Russell Moore must have known when he sang
                                        for the very first time
through the brass-boned monster.
All through the last few nights I have watched you fight for yourself
with the eyes I was warned against opening.
                                You think you are asleep
when you turn off the lights, and we blend into the same
                                hot-skinned sky.
The land called sacrifice is the daughter you never died for and she
stands at the edge of the bed with her slim hand
                                        against your cheek.

116

Your music is a crystal wall with a thousand mouths, kin to trains and
sounds that haven't yet been invented
                                        and you walk back and forth
through it to know that it won't betray you.
And in the last seconds before the breaking light
when you are nearly broken with the secret antelope
of compassion,
                    when the last guardian angel has flown west to the Pacific
to see someone else through their nightly death,
a homefire is slowly kindled in the village of your body.
And the smoke of dawn turns all of your worded enemies
into ashes that will never rise.
Mythic cattle graze in your throat, washing it with milk.
*And you will sing forever.*

# Eloise Klein Healy

## Like a Wick, I Thought, a Woman

Like a wick, I thought, a woman.
No, like smoke from a candle. She was
not burning, but smoke like the shred
that hangs when the fire is pinched out.
There with her shopping cart at Sunset
and North Spring, grey as the dusky November
night. But at third glance, she could have been
a man, bearded and gaunt. A winter pelt of hair.
Who can tell? Something hormonal gone
beyond repair. Like the grocery lot lady
who's grown a goatee. She sings and strokes
it and sings with her head tipped back.
Some star or moon has captured her song.
She sings up at it now through the smoky sky.
A greybeard now, a wisp of wisdom song
and a cigarette she waves through the air
like a wand.

## Moon on the Porch

Moon on the porch thumps his tail when I climb
the stairs. He's got a rock in his mouth, old dog,
and will I play? Old teeth worn into stubs
from carrying rocks. Old moon who limps
as far as we'll walk him. Drinks from the hot
tub when you're not looking, when the moon slides
over the edge of the roof and naked into the water.
I didn't know then this would be a poem to all
my lovers, planted by you in the full moon,
the water running off your breasts, falling
like silver coins into a pool. I didn't know
then how many women I was learning to love.

118

# Lance Henson

## sitting outside in early morning

a single face follows me out of sleep
summers wind through chimes at morning

a white crane lands beyond my sight
near waters edge

having watched a long while
i withdraw under the sound of locusts

a breeze settles like ash
on everything

day breaks open this way


## sketches near youngstown ohio

*for james wright*

over the rough roads of pennsylvania
and ohio
we drive a steady path west

the big dipper and morning star
cast their blessing light
upon us

dawn
in the cradle of a river valley

the fog lifts its gray cover to reveal
the carcasses of two dead deer

two silent places that have fallen upon the earth
at the side of a busy road

somewhere in a deep acre of meadow
the wind passes its morning song
among the flowers

it is there you have left your name


## in january

a single ember in the fireplace
sends a trail of woodsmoke up the chimney

the house grown cold

the clear note of winter on everything


## after a summer fire

foraging for wood in a forest recently burned
charred leaves crackle under the weight of our boots

axe blade so loose it takes four taps
against a tree to keep in place

i pause from cutting

no cicada song here
no wind

i take refuge in the laughter
of a passing crow

# Calvin Hernton

## Mad House

Here is a place that is no place
And here is no place that is a place
A place somewhere beyond time
And beyond the reaches of those who in time
Bring flowers and fruit to this place.
Yet here is a definite place
And a definite time, fixed
In a timelessness of precise vantage
From which to view flowers and view fruit
And view those who come bearing them.

Those who come by Sunday's habit are weary
And kiss us half-foreign but sympathetic;
Spread, eat noisily to crack the unbearable
Silence of this place—
They do not know that something must always
Come from something and that nothing must come
Always from nothing, and that nothing is always

A thing to drive us mad.

# Juan Felipe Herrera

## Foreign Inhabitant

I have lived here, in exile, for seven years.
There was a trial.

It didn't come to nothing.

The papers said I tried to wrap a wire
around a dignitary's neck. I escaped.
But why do I tell you this?

We are all assassins
coveting the warmth inside the jeweler's castle.
I came to America.

I live in the middle of a commoner's quarters,
underground, with a light-skinned and robust Joe Youknowho,
and the unforgiving squint from an abandoned grandmother
at the end of the hallway.

I stay up at night hearing the crackle of the toaster,
the sizzle of tomato with peppers, the President's speech
and on the FM, an old song by Astrud Gilberto.

I write poems and blow smoke rings.
I pull in and feel the scar underneath the left side of my shirt;
it is my wife: smooth, thin, silent, floating, somewhere
around me, far away.

No one obeys the calendar or the clock;
those very loud open-mouthed executioners
of our smallest and secret imaginings.

Not anymore. We go about like the vapor of candles,
attached only to our own whispers.

We hear about suicide squads;
a bomb in the Safeway supermarket or the Golden Gate.
It's funny, now that I am here,
warmth disappears quickly.
Now, I can say this.

Why did I run here?
War inevitably opens all the doors.
My people back home must know this.

There are only a very few at the front of the barracks,
that still believe in the dark blue evening
that will shield us with a star.


## Story & King Blvd: Teen-Age Totems

Skirt fenders on a two-tone Plymouth like the one my uncle Ferni drove to
Mexico City back in '57. At night the street looks like Xmas. Angelina ran
away from the shelter. Her foster mother wants to keep her, but she lost her
license. She got caught with cocaine, the kids said. Angie's boyfriend used to
bring it over. Now, this is hearsay, ok? He got stabbed last week. He said he
was going to support her. I used to want to be a singer. Her grandfather did
things to her for years. She just met her brother who's 19 years old. They told
me he was my uncle. I hate social workers, why don't they leave me alone.
You have to turn yourself in to the shelter, Angie. Maybe when I have my
baby, my mom will be happy. I know she will. And we'll talk and she'll take
care of me. I hate her. She misses you. She hits my sister all the time. She
says it's ok to go out, but, when I come home she calls me a slut. The coun-
selor is looking for your file. But, I am going to have my baby, anytime, now.
What are you going to name him, her? It's going to be a boy. Anthony, or
maybe Carlos. She manipulates you, she knows the system. She can't have
her way. She's still under age. 14. Tell her I have a satellite home for her. As
of now, I have a warrant on her. I used to want to be a singer. Who's that girl
at the bus stop. It's midnight.

## Velvet Baroque/Act

I have never felt so Rococó.
For nearly 15 years I have been an artisan of sorts.

Enduring.
Predictable.
My table has taken an air of diligence.

What happened to my crime report?

My studio is stocked with other's desires,
the umbilicus of love's folly and all the counterfeit
gestures of the would-be modern dancer.

I should lean forward, away
into an open loft with papier-mâché sculptures;
the kid with baggy sox

and purple pants.

I am really an actor. Quite truthfully.
I like to pick up phones and speak
to the Nothing.

You don't have to project.
How did Andy Warhol do it?
My name is Señor K.

I starred in the first run of *Dutchman*.
What did you think?

You should model they kept telling me.
Liars. Ok, I said.
I seemed so natural. The audience
can break your neck.

I am the pick-pocket of Magic
fashioning myself
in front of a mirror
wearing something
I never found, a New York accent, for example.

# Geary Hobson

## Central Highlands, Viet Nam, 1968

### 1

An eagle glides above the plain
where mice scurry in a vortex
of smoke and blood.
Wings dip, soar downward
in a clash
of fire
and upheaval
of earth and bone.

### 2

You will die, Dull Knife,
and your people,
and your vanquisher's descendants
will weep over their father's deeds.

### 3

In the mountains of Viet Nam
the Meo people, too,
will pass
from this world in napalm flashes
and burnt-out hillsides
and all that will be left
to give
will be

the helpless tears
of history future.

4

The eagle flies blindly
into the smoke of his past.

# Richard Hoffman

## Sweat

A man is mowing between the rows of headstones
on a little toy-like tractor. It's hot;
he wipes his face and underneath his cap.
The sun glares off the polished stones.

He hates it—the job, the heat, the flies;
he wanted to be something else.
The sweat on the back of his dark green shirt
could be a black, triangular insignia.

And with his shears, on his hands and knees,
trimming around the crosses, angels, urns,
crawling from stone to stone, he could be
grieving inconsolably for everyone.

## From a Front Window

### 1

There is the city of glass and money,
over there, but here it comes,
closer with every newspaper.
Unidentified lying spokesmen
interpret the same old photos:
the bloody feet of refugees,
the bloody hands of soldiers.
Here comes someone, not a neighbor,
with a clipboard and a calculator.

Where will we grow children and roses?
Where will we grow older?


2


Because mothers still tell children
making ugly faces to be careful
or they will harden into one of them,
I am a little less afraid.

When fathers wipe their children's dirty faces
with handkerchiefs that smell of sweat,
their children do not forget them
easily. I am a gladdened father
learning that, and a calmer son.


3


And lovers' bodies make a clumsy knot
just good enough to mend the net.

# Linda Hogan

## The Truth Is

In my left pocket a Chickasaw hand
rests on the bone of the pelvis.
In my right pocket
a white hand. Don't worry. It's mine
and not some thief's.
It belongs to a woman who sleeps in a twin bed
even though she falls in love too easily,
and walks along with hands
in her empty pockets
even though she has put them in others
for love not money.

About the hands, I'd like to say
I am a tree, grafted branches
bearing two kinds of fruit,
apricots maybe and pit cherries.
It's not that way. The truth is
we are crowded together
and knock against each other at night.
We want amnesty.

Linda, girl, I keep telling you
this is nonsense
about who loved who
and who killed who.

Here I am, taped together
like some old civilian conservation corps
passed by from the great depression
and my pockets are empty.
It's just as well since they are masks

for the soul, and since coins and keys
both have the sharp teeth of property.

Girl, I say,
it is dangerous to be a woman of two countries.
You've got your hands in the dark
of two empty pockets. Even though
you walk and whistle like you aren't afraid
you know which pocket the enemy lives in
and you remember how to fight
so you better keep right on walking.
And you remember who killed who.
For this you want amnesty
and there's that knocking on the door
in the middle of the night.

Relax, there are other things to think about.
Shoes for instance.
Now those are the true masks of the soul.
The left shoe
and the right one with its white foot.


## All Winter

In winter I remember
how the white snow
swallowed those who came before me.
They sing from the earth.
This is what happened to the voices.
They have gone underground.

I remember how the man named Fire
carried a gun. I saw him
burning.
His ancestors live in the woodstove
and cry at night and are broken.

This is what happens to fire.
It consumes itself.

In the coldest weather, I recall
that I am in every creature
and they are in me.
My bones feel their terrible ache
and want to fall open
in fields of vanished mice
and horseless hooves.

And I know how long it takes
to travel the sky,
for buffalo are still living
across the drifting face of the moon.

These nights the air is full of spirits.
They breathe on windows.
They are the ones that leave fingerprints
on glass when they point out
the things that happen,
the things we might forget.


## The Other Side

At sunset
the white horse has disappeared
over the edge of earth
like the sun running from the teeth of darkness.

Fleeing past men who clean weapons
in sudden light, women
breaking eggs in faith
that new ones will grow

radiant in feather cribs
the coyotes watch over.

All the innocent predators!
Even the moon can't stop to rest
in the tree's broken arm,
and at sunset the cows of the field turn away
from the world
wearing a death mask.

White horse.
White horse
I listen for you to return
like morning
from the open mouth of the underworld,
kicking in its teeth.
I listen for the sound of you
tamping fast earth, a testimony
of good luck nailed to hooves.

Even the moon can't stop to rest,
and the broken branch is innocent
of its own death
as it goes on breathing
what's in the air these days,
radiating soft new leaves,
telling a story about the other side of creation.

# Barbara Helfgott Hyett

## The Cigarette Salesman

In winged-tip shoes
and a gray fedora, he is
The Company's Best Man,
his order book bulging with names.
He sells Cuban cigars
for the display case
in the marble lobby
of the Breakers Hotel.

With yellow stained fingers,
he pats the ass of the girl
at the cash register, grinning
his wide, tarnished smile afterwards
as he walks the street, lugging
crumbs and cellophaned samples
into the next-stop luncheonette.
In the leather satchel,
packs and packs of Philip Morris
crush against the Lucky Strike.

His pocket is full
of what he's taken:
mint-flavored toothpicks
for the children who wait
for him to come home at dusk,
too tired for the story
about someplace far,
where, once, a tobacco barge
carried him to a packing job
in the customhouse—peacocks
carved into the wooden portico,
huge ceiling fans churning smoke
as high as he could dream.

## Sunday and the Cigarette Salesman

In the living room where slipcovers
smell of mothballs all summer long
he works in a sleeveless tee-shirt
under the window. Sunday morning artisan,
hammer and nails spread on the sill.
At the other window, an uneven sun
squints through the slats of the blinds.
He sits on a low stool,
replacing a frayed window sash.

Behind him, at the upright dowry piano,
his wife, still in a cotton housecoat,
bedroom slippers flapping time
against her heels.
Her dime-store music played by ear,
her hands riding the ivory keys.

*Saint Lou-ee woman*
he's singing
*with her diamond rings.* Gutturals
edge the window, grind
across the alley where the neighbor
is hanging wash on the roof, holding
him to her eyes, clothespins pressed
shoulder-to-shoulder
around her husband's underwear.
She licks her lips to the song.

His long fingers
ply the snapped cord, eyes dancing
over the arch of her barefoot,
the ankle curve, her calf
taut with reaching.
She flashes her teeth at the man
half out of the window with want.
The woman wants the sun
to be fixed
at ten o'clock high and climbing.

# Lawson Fusao Inada

## John Coltrane

Coltrane's home is the oldest home there is.
It is older than houses; it is older than clothes.
It is older than shelter; it is older than us.

It says so in the scripture of the structure.

There was light; there were the elements.
There came a clearing in the forest.
There came, then, the great encampment.

Oh, there were places to stay, then,
to get out of the wind and the rain.
As we moved on, we took the sky with us.

Then came some lean-to, some little cabin.
The rest is history; the music, testament.

Who knows what else this place has been?
As we moved on, the moon came with us.

Domicile, shrine, mortuary, mosque . . .
Whatever we conducted there was business.
And what it was, was always simultaneous:

a humble cottage, a healer's secular office,
main headquarters of the underground surface . . .

Is that a train I hear?
A call to prayer?
Who walks the constellations?
What river is near?

Whatever this is, it is a house of worship.
This is the temple of the soul and spirit.

This is the temple of all gods, manifest.
This is the temple of the sun and stars.
This is the temple of the abiding reverence.

There. There. There, now. There. There.


## Miles Davis

Miles' house
(quite unexpectedly some say)
is all mirrors.
As his janitor explains:
"Miles looks at himself."
But how to explain
all the exterior walls?—
mirrors, mirrors, mirrors . . .
According to a critic:
"Miles mirrors the times."

Whatever, it's a deceptively
difficult place to find,
since it resembles
exactly what surrounds it,
including the sky.
Learned birds, therefore,
prefer it for perches;
it's the next best thing
to flying.
Plants glory in the reflection.
They lean against it,
like a mother.
And at night, all manner
of moths and fireflies
come to come in contact
with the moon and stars.

Inside, as expected,
Miles is on guard.
After all, the insurance is expensive,
and grit from your feet

can mar the mirrored floors.
The lighting is, of course,
very definitely *muted*.
It even seems to have that
"Miles Davis sound"—
sensuous, soft, elusive
edges exuding the fragrance of nuances.
The source of light, however,
is naturally deceptive,
the warming, receptive rays of the sun
radiating indivisibly
from all corners, floors . . .
Thus, even open spaces
inspire your undivided attention.

Where did he go? When did he exit?
Is he watching from what?
Is he bored with this visit?
Then here comes that
Miles Davis music.
It is a visible feeling.
It sifts over surfaces,
it drifts over mirrors—
floors, walls, corners, ceilings,
and on outside
where it takes to the air . . .

Miles! Miles! Miles!
It echoes.
It sings in your ears!
It swings through your system—
reflecting, reflecting, reflecting . . .
Mirrors and mirrors and mirrors . . .

You go on forever.
You are both far and close.
There you are, a multitude.
Here you are, eye to eye, alone.

What does this mean? Do you know?

"Miles is the mirror of the soul."

# Colette Inez

## Old Woman out of Iowa

Insolent days of light and clouds.
Sometimes she stared like someone who knew
the time had come to nothing, blamed me
for frazzling her nerves,
cussed out her son, Ray,
for marrying so soon
after Ruthie died of booze.

"Shut your mouth and stand up straight,"
she'd say to me. I slumped and called her witch
under my breath. That summer didn't
give a damn about my pleas for calm.
I hunched over books, mystery, romance,
a world of mist and balustrades.

When Ray took an axe to our door,
she stood on two canes near the bed,
ratty housecoat, grizzled hair.
I hid. The door caved in. She stared
him down. Later, he disappeared into
the junklot of drunken men.

Her hands were folded just so in the casket.
The summer wind combed back the leaves.
She was my witness, that old woman
out of Iowa. She held her balance
with two canes and a midwestern will to stay
upright. Today, standing over her grave,
I throw my shoulders back in a grudging salute.

## Red August Letter

Dear Friend:
The day you brought me geraniums,
my period came. That night I had a red dream,
red walls, lamps. You were a photographer
in a darkroom developing shots I couldn't
quite make out. I asked how you balanced
opposing needs. You shrugged and lifted
pictures out of a chemical bath.

In the photo you left of the party, who is
the feral-looking poet in the rumpled suit?
Woman hater? Once I would have memorized his poems.
The rain goes on. I've read your note, its chaste,
familiar script on a monogrammed blue page. I write.
My paper laps up ink. Stamps curl. A vague
taste of stickum lingers in my mouth.

Slack hours. Do you ever imagine the atoms
of your watch pulsing in a fading light?
Take a stand, intones my clock from its orderly
frontier. I resolve to reconcile odds and ends,
to inspect, put things out of sight, receive
the house-god, give him loose-skinned oranges,
an offering for auspicious news.

Was it last spring, after we'd found the cardinal's
nest fastened to a branch of pine, we spoke of ways
to stave off birth? What I didn't say was that
my scrap of a child sometimes floats in the back
of my head like a sea-creature, open-mouthed
as if it were startled or in pain to learn its
name would not be called.

Why hadn't I known of the Zulu woman
who counted stars in her labor from a hole
in the ceiling of her hut? Would knowing it
have changed the fact I didn't have the spunk
to watch the tight bud open to a rose,

giving birth to a red dream, to alpha, a letter
in August, giving birth to fingerprints
in a spectrum of light?

Tonight Mars and Venus are aligned in the summer
sky. Come with your prints and films. All week
opulent sunsets have fallen on soaked roads.
Forecasters say nothing we haven't heard.
I want to hear your reflector dream, your daughter
dream, to be brought into communion with old ghosts.

# Lonny Kaneko

## Wild Light

We stand before the long building
others call "latrine," my father and I,
in the dark, looking where stars
should shine but where storm clouds roll
on themselves as they do in time-lapse
photography. Rain strikes like little nails;
a jagged torch catches a still photograph:
our faces upturned to catch the rain
catch the light. The smell of it erases
the new-lumber of our room, the dirt
and plaster, the new urine on new concrete.
In seconds thunder echoes back. Again
and again, lightning follows lightning.
Each flash rips the Idaho sky.
Like folding chairs, we've been installed
in unfinished rooms. We struggle through dust
or snow or rain to pee. My parents have
carried me through the upheaval of rifles,
baggage tags, catcalls and the daily journeys
of the mind into semi-arid flats,
until this electric moment. Midnight,
and the child's mind rises. The yellow balloon
they have carried me in pops like thunder.
My father's hand wilts in mine. I am alone
in the storm's passage, dispossessed of bed
and apple trees. Each toy, each dust wisp,
each tricycle track that charts my universe
is shattered by the sharp squeal
of light, the last bark of thunder.

That's when light, like a wild hare
darting through sage, in a rattle-
struck leap, lifts itself free
of the damp sack of land. In the eye

141

of light is a will sky-wide and deep
as darkness. My leap, brief as the hole
lightning makes in the sky, is free
of barbed wire and any brimstone cup
of words. I am pursued by the mystery
that rushes across the desert
after its own blinding imagination.

## Bailey Gatzert: The First Grade, 1945

Miss Riley stands above me, fading fast
beneath the porcelain light that frames her face.
Her finger, raised to God, declares each word,
each careful pencil mark must fill the void
between the faded lines. She measures us
the way she measures words like *brother, house,*
like *sister, sky,* and *dog,* the way she measured
Stanley by standing him against the chalkboard.

The words are always only hers. She draws
the list and keeps the rules. The sky is bruised
but never green, a house can be magenta
and sister pink but never yellow. She matches
objects to their hues. We learn her world,
but she is never part of ours. She would
never walk down alleys, never visit
one room homes too poor to have a guest,

or running water, a stove, or ice. She hawks
us in the class. No boy dares laugh or talk.
An easel slants its errant legs as if
to trip the unaware; we tiptoe past it.
(Three long snows, a gift from Franklin D.,
has taught us how, without apology,
to live behind barbed wire and journey home.)
We know to quiet trembling mouths and hands.
Words contain our thoughts. They tell just who
we really are, or camouflage the fool,
the quiet stranger who lies behind the smile.
One day I whisper, "Benjo . . . Benjo." I try

142

to tell her what I mean. "What did you say?"
Her question rocks the room and laughter sails
on wings about my ears. She checks her list.
No *benjo* there. "O-benjo!" I can't lose

control: frustration pools a cadmium stain
across the floor. Miss Riley turns, her silence
a naked finger: enemy! I've mixed
American and Japanese. She rakes
her memory—does she hear the dying cries
of boys who toppled easels, erased the sky,
then grew to manhood on the way to war?
My hand's raised to heaven. I'm here. I'm here.


## Beasts from the Heart

They're here tonight as they always are,
waiting for us to enter their private dark,
their muzzles gray with the digging
that pervades their lives.
They are content to spend their lives
in afternoons that hold no more than dreams.
When we sleep, they test their voices
against the night's blind disorder.

I enter the cave, and the mind's voice
heats the soft fat of my childhood.
My stutter shuts off the world
and insures my isolation.
Nothing exists. The eye
mirrors the self. Where
does the beast begin?
As the central figure in the play
it enters disguised
in a housedress, long black hair
rolled into a bun, a tongue
sharp as a row of needles.

In December my mother snarled
when she meant to smile. I curled

143

bear-like in the cave of their lives.
I have sniffed the dim reaches
of the undergrowth.
I have seen the tunnels of moles and gophers.
The blind wanderings of prescient worms
have led to the central root that fed
the barbed circle of her words.

It is enough that the beast
should roll in it and dust my nose in it—
this abstraction of dirt I wear?
The cold is not cold until I admit it;
heat is never sweltering until the mind perspires;
and pain—the cut does not bleed until I look
for blood; the body is too ready
to comply with what the mind desires.

Outside the chain-link
preserve is a world for hunters
who reserve the hours between midnight
and dawn to drift into the lives
that surround them. I feel the brush
of wilderness against my thigh.

Midnight! The people who love
me enter their own nightmares.
The chains are lifted,
and I revert to the invisible hunter.
When I howl the world descends.

# *Maurice Kenny*

## Sacrifice

*For Joe & Carol*

wolf tracks
on the snow

I follow between
tamarack and birch

cross the frozen creek
dried mulleins
with broken arms
stand in shadows

tracks move uphill
deeper into snowed conifers

I hurry to catch up
with his hunger

cedar sing in the night
of the Adirondacks
he huddles under bent
red willow
panting

I strip in the cold
wait for him to approach
he has returned
to the mountains

partridge drum
in the moonlight
under black spruce

145

# Black River—Summer 1981

*For Patti-Lyn*

The evening river carries no sound . . .
not the bark of this fox whose skull
weights my hand,
nor the wind of this hawk
feather tucked into the buttonhole of my shirt.

Rivers grumble and hiss and gurgle;
they roar and sing lullabies;
rivers rage and flow and dance
like unseen wind;
in the dark they carry the eyes
of stars and footprints of deer.

    I have slept on your arm
    dawn sweetening my mouth,
    stiff in limb
    and rose to your morning song.

    I have watched geese fly over,
    eels slither downstream,
    bullheads defy rapids,
    spiders ripple waves
    in trapped inlets along the shore,
    fireflies light paths
    from murky banks
    to mysterious islands
    where witches live.

    I have studied your waters:

    Daydreamed my watch to listen,
    to feel your tremble,
    to learn your summer,
    touch your winter,
    and be content.

# Rudy Kikel

## From "Autographs, 1955"

### 1. Rudy Kikel

"My album's open, come and see.
What, won't you waste a line on me!
Write but a thought, a word or two,
that memory may revert to you."

No reverting to me, dear,
the ghost—or the flesh—of yourself
    in the future, who you were
dying then I guess to become.

Memory must leap forward
to meet me, although if it could
    it would not be memory
but premonition, which you had

already. Now in the way
of a "line on" you, I shall first
    have to get one—perhaps from
your album page of *Favorites*.

*Athlete:* "Mickey Mantle." *Book:*
"Bible." Conventional wisdom
    only, there. But then how could
you have come up with smart answers

when the questions for you
were all wrong? Take *Chum*, for instance.
    Whatever Kevin, Richie,
Frank were—"Sister," Conspirator,
    Savior?—chums they were not.

Here is something. Song: "Pepper-Hot
    Baby." That would be yourself,
burning. Also this. Sport: "Swimming."

    No competition there! Sport
would provide even more relief
    at St. John's, where to enter
the pool, boys stripped out of their briefs

    completely. Little sissy,
sweetheart, you begin to come back
    to me. My "thought?" It is that
nothing is wasted and no self

    gone. While I live, you also
shall be kept alive, because you
    by being yourself let me
live. We were—I was—always one.


2.  Laureen Heckermann

    "On this page of pretty white,
        Only an angel would dare to write."

    When just before the awards
were granted Sister pointed out
    that we would be receiving
General Excellency medals

    that year, she made official
merely what everybody knew:
    academically you and
I were the crowned head of our class.

    I emceed "Alumni Night,"
you gave a Valedictory
    Address, the wonderfully
controlled pauses in which said more

    clearly perhaps than did words
that yours was a star ascendant.

**148**

You left a decidedly
blue-collar Glendale, and I was

invited to follow, on
the occasions of your catered
    affairs, which I never missed,
until—having made on leaving

one the blunder of shoving
my tongue in your mouth—I was not
    invited back. Then, whereas
I joined St. John's "animal frat,"

you became a "Zeta girl"
and drifted out of my orbit.
    I see you are not listed
in the new Class Directory:

are you out of everyone's
orbit now? I remember Lee
    Pritchett's suddenly under
the table pulling my leg hairs

at another Jamaica
Estates party—to see if I
    had any! My kind of girl,
I thought. Anyway, no angel.

# Kevin Killian

## The Push

When I reached fourteen like grey
Gibraltar rock there you lounged before me

in your furnished room by flats
on the railroad's edge.

With the miffed look of the St.
Bernard, who slogs through storm
only to find the traveller already
frozen, I turned fourteen and found

you. Still I saw a ray of hope.

When I turned fourteen there you were
a ditch so wide, so filled with white
sluggish life, I said "Hope I pass out
before I puke" to someone unseen.
Nice apartment.

                    Late day
we heard whistles and vamps from trains
going off somewhere out of century
out towards smoky nightmail.

                    Cutting school
I heard whistles from stockyards and
the weasely cry of cows, getting their
insides sucked out by your house.
Kind of a Chicago story out there.

                    Late day
and trains shunting by your back cellar

stairs, and your red geraniums wilting
in your windowbox. Pull the curtains

                You
made me drink coffee, said I'd shoot up
faster at the age of wet shot seen hot
zone age of fourteen.

                You
put something in my coffee: only
Cremora or some kind of bachelors'
sex dust? "Spanish fly" went buzzing
in my head; *this is so grown up.*

                Lying
like Hell I shook my head. I walked
around a potted palm on the floor
that looked like a bed, that you watered
with coffee.

Over a trunk you bent and the soap
operas dimmed out like the train's
two lights in *Love in Vain*;

you sent your hands to a floor
overrun by dustmice—a movie star
honored by Grauman's Chinese.

Why can't we do this all our
lives I said up in the clouds
in your coldwater cellar!

Oh—you said kind of discontented
push-baby-push-baby-push—

# Irena Klepfisz

## Fradel Schtok

*Yiddish writer. B. 1890 in Skale, Galicia. Emigrated to New York in
1907. Became known when she introduced the sonnet form into Yiddish
poetry. Author of* Erzeylungen [Stories] *(1919), a collection in Yiddish.
Switched to English and published* For Musicians Only *(1927).
Institutionalized and died in a sanitarium around 1930.*

*"Language is the only homeland."*

Czeslow Milosz


They make it sound easy:     some disjointed
sentences     a few allusions     to
mankind.     But for me     it was not
so simple     more like     trying
to cover the distance     from here
to the corner     or between two sounds.

Think of it:     *heym*     and     *home*     the meaning
the same     of course     exactly
but the shift     in vowel     was the ocean
in which I drowned.

I tried.     I did     try.
First held with Yiddish     but you
know     it's hard.     You write     *gas*
and     *street*     echoes back.
No resonance.     And—let's face it—
memory falters.
You try to keep track of the difference
like *got* and *god*     or *hoyz* and *house*
but they blur     and you start using
*alley*     when you mean *gesele*     or *avenue*
when it's a *bulevar*.

And before you know it
you're on     some alien path

152

standing    before a brick house
the doorframe    slightly familiar.
Still    you can't place it
exactly.    Passers-by    stop.
Concerned    they speak    but you've
heard    all this    before    the vowels
shifting    up and down    the subtle
change    in the gutteral sounds
and now    it's nothing more
nothing    more    than babble.
And so    you accept it.
You're lost.    This time    you really
don't know    where you are.

Land or sea    the house floats before you.
Perhaps you once sat    at that window
and it was home    and looked out
on that *street* or *gesele*. Perhaps
it was a dead end    perhaps a short cut.
Perhaps not.
A movement by the door. They stand there
beckoning    mouths open and close:
*Come in! Come in!*    I understood    it was
a welcome. *A dank! A dank!*
I said    till I hear the lock
snap    behind me.

## Cactus

*For my mother*
*Rose Perczykow Klepfisz*

The pot itself was half the story.
A yellow ceramic dime store knickknack
of a featureless Mexican
with a large sombrero    pushing a wagon
filled with dirt.

The cactus was the other half.
Self-effacing    it didn't demand much

which was just as well
since she had no spare time
for delicate cultivation.
Used to just the bare essentials
it stood on our kitchen windowsill
two floors above the inhospitable soil
and neither flourished     grew
nor died.

I'd catch her eyeing it
as she stood     breathless
broiling our dinner's minute steaks
her profile centered in the windowframe.
She understood     the meaning     of both pot
and plant     still would insist there was
something extra     the colors yellow
green     or as she once explained
in her stiff     night school English:
"It is always     of importance to see
the things aesthetical."

# Etheridge Knight

## Circling the Daughter

*For Tandi*

You came / to be / in the Month of Malcolm,
And the rain fell with a fierce gentleness,
Like a martyr's tears,
On the streets of Manhattan when your light was lit;
And the City sang you Welcome. Now I sit,
Trembling in your presence. Fourteen years
Have brought the moon-blood, the roundness,
The girl-giggles, the grand-leaps.
We are touch-tender in our fears.

*You break my eyes with your beauty:*
*Ooouu-oo-baby-I-love-you.*

Do not listen to the lies of old men
Who fear your power,
Who preach that you were "born in sin."
A flower is moral by its own flowering.
Reach always within
For the Music and the Dance and the Circling.

O Tandiwe, by Beloved of this land,
Your spring will come early and
When the earth begins its humming,
Begin your dance with men
With a Grin and a Grace of whirling.
Your place is neither ahead nor behind,
Neither right nor left. The world is round.
Make the sound of your breathing
A silver bell at midnight
And the chilling wet of the morning dew . . .

*You break my eyes with your beauty:*
*Ooouu-oo-baby-I-love-you.*

# A Black Poet Leaps to His Death

*For mbembe milton smith*

was it a blast to the balls dear brother
with the wind ringing in the ear
that great rush against the air
that great push
                into the universe

you are not now alone mbembe
of the innocent eyes     sadder
than a mondays rain     it is i
who hear your crush of bone
           your splatter of brain
           your tear of flesh
on the cold chicago stone

           and my october cry
when the yellow moon is ringed with blood
of children dead in the lebanese mud
     is as sharp as a kc switchblade
your pain is a slash across my throat
i feel a chill     can the poet belie
the poem
     old revolutionaries never die
it is said
     they just be born again
(check chuck colson and his panther from folsom)
but you are *dead*
mbembe     poetman in the home of the brave
the brown leaves whister across you grave

but it must have been a rush     a great gasp
        of breath
        the awesome leap to your death
o poet of the blood and bone
        of the short song
        and serious belief
i sing you release

# Geraldine Kudaka

## Suburban Dream

The smog starts rolling in about 5 o'clock.
I'm up before the alarm. I make him breakfast,
eggs over easy. He leaves. I wash my hair
swallowing gulps of warm clean water.
I dress quickly, sliding the slip, the skirt,
over my head. Standing before the mirror,
my fingertips spy out my breasts.

    You'll call these little hills, and dig in,
    burrowing trails along the flesh.

I was told they can smell another man on you,
and yet, I'll worry open the door and
silence the fearful screams. I'll go through
the motions, swearing this will be the last time,
the last time.

A bomb will consume my brain.
You'll root in, planting your seed. My breasts
will grow wildflowers, my legs spindly roots.
I'll say "yes," hating this body that twists
and turns. Loving you will be a slow death.
I'll make you leave, screaming inside my lungs.

I'll want you again. I'll dream about your seed
spreading like a valley of weeds.
I'll make my legs walk, reminding my body
there's only room enough for one man.
And when he comes home, my hands will worm
their way through his hair.

# Giving Up Butterflies

*Fresno, 1948*

The others stand in their imported
ready-made wear.
I stand apart, my carefully dressed hair
coiffed above a starched, white dress.

I suck in my stomach,
pulling flat the tell-tale months,
that single moment
when mattress springs dug into my back.

i

The placenta came out intact.
I had bruises for months afterwards.
The necklace you gave me hung off my door,
the shimmering light that danced off
was all that you left.

ii

Under a barren walnut tree,
my shovel propped up the newborn bark.
I sat starring at the empty hole, the corn
flour sack, and that morning's paper.

For months on end, I sat rocking time
back and forth.
The shell of my life cracked into two distinct
moments, back and forth.
Back and forth.

My bare soles rubbed one spot
on the rickety floor. My arms were

hard and stiff, my legs bare and hollow.
I rocked,
waiting for god knows what,
back and forth.


iii

My mother screamed, "Turn off the water!
What do you think we are? Rich?"
Clicking the lock in place, I paid her no
attention.

I waited until she left, then dressed
in my Sunday best.
Standing on the porch, I caught a butterfly
and tore off its wings.
I buried its wings under the maple tree.
The dull sparkles in the cold, brown soil
forgot to shine.


iv

Inside my body, an unknown surgeon
has cauterized my pride.
My hurt betrays me. I can't look
up, my eyes are glued to the polished
oak, the leather shoes.

The smoking laughter of the crowd fills
the air with an unpleasant
smell. You glide by, your feet so
swift, so sure,
packs my heart into a tiny earthen knot.

With one hand covering my eyes, the other
carrying my pride, I walk out.
In the autumn night, I feel the frost
of winter.
Soon it will be spring.


159

# Joan Larkin

## Blackout Sonnets

Something happened I couldn't have told you then.
He was dark, with a beak like Uncle Ben's,
another salesman in a suit. Barry, my music teacher's son—
a senior, hot when I was twelve, Book One
propped on the instrument.
Now I was eighteen. My mother was intent
about my hem and hair. On her knees,
mouth full of pins, she spit out sharp advice:
*Don't overdo the makeup. Face*
*facts: you've got my hips.* She was amazed
a plausible, tall Jew would date
her daughter. I was damaged goods. Too late
to do me any good, she'd said last year,
*You're nothing, if you've lost your precious treasure.*

You're nothing, if you've lost your precious treasure.
So I guess I gave him nothing, on the sofa
in his parents' finished basement (big tv,
plush carpet, bar), listening New Year's eve
to his favorite Gershwin—which we had to hear
twice. Zero degrees, I felt numb about the year
1957. His folks, a blur
of blue cigar smoke and a full-length fur,
were climbing into the Caddy as we drove in:
*Goodnight*—I was unprepared. She still looked grim
as when I hadn't practiced, which was most
of the time. Barry, the conscientious host,
opened two bottles of sparkling Cold Duck
one after the other—the suave fuck.

One after the other, the suave fuck
followed by fake champagne. I wasn't struck
by the way I took his cues; only his taste

160

appalled me. Eighteen, I was a wine-snob, based
on one date with a transfer student from Paris.
Cold Duck fluorescent in my blood, black dress
hiked to my hips, my pale pink synthetic
panties spilled on the rug, his tireless prick
battering my numbed entrance—I couldn't say
whether or not I wanted it that way.
For all I know, we would have gone someplace—
dancing, a movie—if, in my half-a-voice,
I'd said, *No more thanks.* Or *What are your plans?*
Whichever, I was in his hands.

Whichever, I was in his hands—
what shit. I wanted him inside my pants.
I knew my lines and hurried through them. Once
drunk, I could direct him, no coy hints,
to close the coffin and then nail me in—
that was the point. Fucking put a lid on pain
like nothing since the rubber cone of ether
on my nose and mouth that night last year.
Saline injection, hot curette in my womb,
blood in the toilet, mother screaming in my room—
the whole damned family was in on it.
Brother, cousin—all of them suffered the secret.
Now Barry flickered and passed out.
Had either of us come? I was in a blackout.

Had either of us come? I was in a blackout.
It was two when I woke up in the Buick on Route
Nine. I stared at the immaculate floor,
carpeted to match dark maroon leather
upholstery. My high heels pierced the shag.
I fished inside my black patent bag
for keys and hoped my mother was in bed.
Barry drove without turning his head.
My pants were soaked. I shivered, though the heat
was blasting. Queasy—*We didn't even eat*—
I clung to my cold keys and stared at signs
and Barry's profile, trying to read his mind.

And in a tone he might have meant to soften,
he said, *Do you do this sort of thing often?*

He said, *Do you do this sort of thing often?*
*No*—I could barely say it. My face stiffened.
It sickens me even now, remembering this:
I had been hoping for a goodnight kiss.
Skidding on new snow, the Buick turned
my corner. Barry clammed up. The cold burned
as he opened the door on my side, courteous,
distant: he had had nothing to do with this.
I grabbed his cashmere sleeve and climbed the icy
steps to the squat brick house I
hated; my folks had moved here right
after the abortion. September, a soft night,
Uncle's knife scraped out my next-of-kin.
Now I drank anything and slept with everyone.

I drank anything and slept with everyone
and kept my mouth shut about the abortion.
I hardly remember 1957—
I stopped speaking to my closest friend
when her boyfriend called me up and said, *I want
your doctor's name.* His sleeve soft, my cunt
sore, we climbed the stairs to 7-B.
Mom opened the door and stared at me
as if I were a mirror. Was my dress
zipped only part way up? Barry glanced at us,
looking supremely sane, said a smooth *Goodnight,*
and left. Her laugh a snort, *You're good and late!*
she said, and *Will he ask you out again?*—
and something happened I couldn't have told you then.

# Meridel Le Sueur

## Budded with Child

Before your cry
                I never heard a cry,
Headless ghost I rode the prairies,
The bodyless head screaming after me.
Skeleton, I searched for rose and flesh,
Lamenting in bereaved villages
Howling in stone cities
I gave berries to strangers
I gave them fruits
                I gave them fruits
For stones and bones and broken words.
In the place where crying begins
The place of borders, the place of the enemy
I begot you, child
Before you I did not know flowers
                out of snow,
Or milk of meadows out of drouth.
Before your cry I never heard a cry,
Or globular breast and milk without summons.
Exiled I cried along the rivers
                caged in time and loss,
Empty pod I longed for winged seeds.
Till merged in earth's agony of birth
                leapt bridge
                struck lyre
Impaled on earth and fleshes spring,
                budded with child.
Before you child I never knew the breast of milk
                the arm of love
                the kerneled grain of groats
Before your face I never saw a face descending
                down my belly to time's horizon
breast and skin multiplied into multitude
                and benevolence.

# James Lewisohn

## For My Wife
## 1936–1974

What I was     you called
into being.
You named me as you brought
        Things into Creation.

The Sabbath and its bread
Fall with the falling of your Flesh
        And we danced
in each other as the only way
Flesh becomes Spirit.

What lost Country are you in
My sister and my bride
        Where are you
Where am I.
Distance from you is like
the last light from a dead star
whose path     empties     empties . . .

Inside that wedding ring
our blood lies locked
in a chalice mixed with each
day and every night

All Women All Men All Children
        Are you to Me
Our very dreams inseparable
Grief is a stone that leaves no shadow
Or like the one Rose Lisa left me
the Water evaporates and the Rose puts
down its darkening head     until it Falls away

Petal by petal as the last farland
of its leaf    divides.

And as you watered the plants—talking
to them Dina, her ripe finger
tested their gravity.
                    Soon the house filled
                    With fragrance.
How important that was.

Onion faltered in your garden
but I stood    watching    watching
because you gave them much care
though that garden 5 by 5
was    built on ledge.

Never the impossible, Roslyn, for you.
Nothing escaped its Chance.


## Going Home

*After a painting by Michael Willis*

Only a hint of light reflected in the snow
far off homes their fires impossible to reach.
The faint rose-colored rush seen briefly now
and then flickering as though a path were impossible.
And soon the colorless, soulless melancholy period
of night approaches. The sky tinted with an
afterglow, the last illumination of the falling
snow its promised prints diminishing. Here the brush
pointing toward a mirage more dream
than desire. Still to follow the last light turning
in its dust. The trees, houses torched by the obscured
breath of twilight. And I remember we had been there
once, had stayed an hour a year many years.

Now I walk through the painting to the never nearer
lights my last imaginings and yours.

And just before sleep it is seen more like the myopic
birds whose wings know the winds path instinctually.
It is not stated. It leaves its traces empty
with our vacancy.
Somewhere someone is going home in the blue cold
afternoon . . .


## Now It Is Time

My son squirms in the pit of his shoes
as he grows into another face.
The year deepens     I look up
and my daughter walks in her woman's body
still the undiscovered child.
She hides her nakedness from us
for her body is too new a thing
to be let out. Nothing I can do will matter now
Winter moves down the valley
stripping the fields of their last fruit,
I touch you in the night
and we grow into our death like an other coat.

Words change from the mouth like benedictions
Now it is time to feed the young birds
Now it is time to build a last house
Not it is time to put food into the earth
giving back the earth its promise.

This is a time to be wise and perfect
This is a time to clarify the light
This is a time to speak softly to one another
as though each word were spoken for the first time
It is a time for letting go and for being near

        again     and     again.

# Stephen Shu-Ning Liu

## Homecoming for April

You wake to the bloodiest month of the year.
Newspaper says that farm dogs brought home
human hands from the desert. A man stabbed his
wife and child and left them on the floor.
But we'll find a shelter for you, April, my
little sparrow arriving in spring storms.

We're not too far from the riverbanks,
where your grandfather fished his red-tail carps.
We're not too far from the sycamore grove,
where snowy egrets established their colonies.
Evening winds swing at us, full of clover scents.
Clouds float about like golden pagodas.
Arise from your mother's arms, my girl.
Look at our garden in cherry blossoms,
listen to those swallows in the eaves.
I see window lights, I see bright chandeliers
in the main hall. The Door God leans over, smiling,
the phoenix gazes down from the lintel.
Old folks are out there to greet us.
A red carpet, they say, is for a son's arrival,
but a green one for a daughter.

On my right stands your grandfather in his best
garment as if he had come for a wedding;
hardly can he remove his eyes from your face
yet limp, yellowish at birth. On my left
sighs deep your grandmother who lowers her head.
"Welcome home, April," she murmured; "I had
sometimes wished you were a boy to sustain
our family line. Ah April, April . . ."

"Dry your eyes, Mother," I plead. "No harsh word,
although your proverb says that 'to store crops

for times of famine, to breed a son for old age.'
Such saying is now stale. Aunt Li, your sister, had
a son, the spoiled brat, the opium pit frequenter.
You had sons, but I left home before the Revolution;
Chung Chu was gone when you lay in bed, dying.
Remember those who made you a box-coffin, those who
dug you a mud bed in the cornfield. They were daughters,
daughters. Sons are like mountain hawks:
they grew up and hurried away, affected by evil stars.

Therefore, be content. Embrace your daughter-in-law
for her being kind to your son. Pour blessings on
April's head and see your own images in her forehead.

What would you say about the baby's mouth, Father?
Does it not remind you of the lily bud you
used to paint? Our child arrives in the year of Horse.
A good sign. Heaven may send Spirits to protect us.

Rarely we have time to meet like this.
Leave your tombs unoccupied by the hillside.
Morning will not come. No light breaks in the sky.
The rainstorm has hushed all roosters in the field."


## Chung Shin

Chung Shin, my little brother, left us
after he had seen nine springs.
It was morning, a sunny day,
the ricefields outside the window
were green and full of joyful sparrows.

Then came the priest in black robes,
with ancient instruments of music.
Days and nights they stood before a row
of haunting candle flames and sang
their scriptures with never changing

sleepy tune, as if they were asking
favors for my brother from gods in heaven.

After Chung Shin's soul was saved
by the blood of a rooster,
my father brought from the village
a paper carriage and horse, with a paper
lantern and paper driver, and burned them
in the graveyard, in order that my brother
might find his way home in the night.
We burned, too, a thousand paper dollars,
so that he might have something to spend.
Lastly my mother burned a paper kite,
for my brother's favorite sport was to fly
a kite in the spring wind.

I saw my mother dry her eyes with a white
handkerchief, I heard my father groan
as he walked to and fro, biting his fist.
I watched the ashes dancing by the cypress.
I smelled the fresh earth and herbs.
I felt the chilly evening air; and I knew
we would go home and leave Chung Shin here
behind a stone. And the day he left us:
it was morning, a sunny day.
The ricefields outside the window
were green and full of joyful sparrows.

# George Ella Lyon

## Rhody

What I have is an image
an outline in the smokehouse door
arms raised above your thick body
cutting down hams for the funeral dinner.
Everyone gone to the churchhouse
ocean of words washing it
bleak as bone.

They made you stay
though it was your man
heavy in the pine box.
His children forced you
as if in a fairy tale
to prepare them all his goods
to strip yourself of him
and the house of you.
All the weight of them in their worn black suits
the smell in dresses that cut under the arms
laid on you like an iron.

So while they pulled
diamond notes from the hymnal
you worked your old ways—
smokehouse to porch,
pump to castiron stove.
You put your hand
under the plump heat of chickens
gathering one last time
the live stones.

# The Foot-Washing

*"I wouldn't take the bread and wine if I didn't wash feet."*

Old Regular Baptist

They kneel on the slanting floor
before feet white as roots,
humble as tree stumps.
Men before men
women before women
to soothe the sourness
bound in each other's journeys.
Corns, callouses, bone knobs
all received and rinsed
given back clean
to Sunday shoes and hightops.

This is how they prepare
for the Lord's Supper,
singing and carrying a towel
and a basin of water,
praying while kids put soot
in their socks—almost as good
as nailing someone in the outhouse.

Jesus started it: He washed feet
after Magdalen dried His ankles
with her hair. "If I wash thee not,
thou hast no part with me."

All servants, they bathe
flesh warped to its balance.
God of the rootwad,
Lord of the bucket in the well.

## Cousin Ella Goes to Town

Now you have to promise
you won't breathe a word of this.
It was after Brian died.
You know I got me a little insurance money
and I said to myself, Eller,
what kind of life have you had
and what are you likely to get
and you know the answer to that.
Not much.

Seemed like all I'd ever done
was dump pennies from a jar.
Brian left me just enough
to stay on in this house
sewing and tending other people's kids
fading out like an old TV.
So I took a hard look.
And do you know what I did?

I went to Louisville.
Yes sir, I got on the Greyhound bus
rode right there
and took a taxi to the Galt House
and for four days
I had me a room
and I pretended
to be somebody else.

Lord, children, I ate the best food
went to dress stores and picture shows
I even called my name different.
And do you know
I got so high and mighty
with my new hairdo—
I had the yellow scared out of this wad
got me a city style—
that on the third night
right before the Icecapades
I was trying on this hat

and I saw my face all gaudy in that mirror
and my freckled hands with peach polish on each nail
and I took to crying
for all the world like Brian had died again.

I grabbed a washrag
and scrubbed my face.
I snatched them bobby pins out of my hair
and brushed it till my scalp
stung like fire.
And honey I got out of there.

By the time the bus let me off
I was plumb out of tears.
I just marched in
put my pocketbook down—
I'd left everything but a raincoat
at the hotel—
I rolled down my stocking
heated up some soup
sat in my chair
and read the Sunday School lesson.
Next morning I tried
to wear that coat to church
but you know it never fit me right
at all.

# J. D. McClatchy

## Wells River

We went along a way we'd gone before,
This time alone—up, against the lash
Of a stream bed where in spring, fools-thaw
Past, the cold year pours down out of itself
The way the will moves toward the term
It has elected, but then of course was dry,
Needled by fall to a dull gloss on itself
That lapped the fieldstone, the fern-locks.
I'd knelt to pick apart a cone of chrysalis.

I mention the details to remind you
Of the give-and-take. You were scuffing
At mossdown, pointing to changes swollen
With growth and decay but no quickening choice,
And to a pair of braided, fluent birches.
"Why aren't *we* alone more often?" Words
That, when I look up too quickly still,
Make me see double to where you stood.
I mean I am *here*, and at the same time *then*,
Your hand as suddenly in mine as I'd reached up,
And the sense of a life together that sounds
A counterforce of wavering,
That change of mind this incline of months
Sends back and forth and back again.

And, as today I woke in the hammock,
Late sunlight daydreaming beside me,
My arm dangling over the side, elbow-deep,
It seemed the way before us had become
a kind of inlet, a needle-eye inlet
On the river, us both a boy in his skiff,
With a basket of food, his retriever.
(What had I been dreaming of before?
What calm regrets, anticipations

Of more than was reflected in some deep
Or exaggerated swerve of light on my face?)
He was moored to a swayback willow.
If setting out, I could have reached down
To loosen the rope, as any friend might
Who had (—I had) our walk in mind.

# Wilma Elizabeth McDaniel

## Note Slipped Under a Door

Lawrence Dooley:
   I have heard the
   altar fires
   are burning dangerously low

   Please light one candle for me
   Surely we can agree
   on something
   as white as beeswax
   on something as pure as
               flame

## Calendars

Some people are good at
remembering milestones
      they recall
   she was married in '27
   he was killed in '44

RANONA never could read
      calendars
   but she is positive
   of tearing off ribbons
   at the age of five
that she cut all strings at
      seventeen

and dumped august into the
   lap of winter
   when she was thirty


## Night Treasures

Sleep
  keeps me waiting
so I stand at the window
and watch night
turn small green pears
to silver
they hang like rare treasures
   I dare not touch
   from a tree
   I never saw before


## Definition

Poets
are queer people
and no one knows
it better
than the girl who walked
  on the long red road
  fought its heat
  kicked its dust
when blessed rain
rolled it into thin clay dolls
  and left it only once
  to hide in bushes
when Gypsies passed

## U.F.W. Pickets on Old Highway 99

Two disciples
went on their way after
    the Resurrection

    Rejoicing to walk in
    cast off shoes
all the way to Delano
    Easter eggs in their
    denim pockets

# Naomi Long Madgett

## Images

### 1

One student (white),
leading a class discussion
of *Native Son*
and running out of things to say,
asked, "How would you feel
if you encountered Bigger Thomas
on a dark street
late at night?"

Another student (black, astute)
countered: "How
would you know it was
Bigger Thomas?"

### 2

I pictured him as muscular,
dull-eyed and dense, his sullen scowl,
skin color, maze of hair
and criminal demeanor defining
my most horrendous nightmare

How can I reconcile
that image
with this tender yellow
boy who could have been
my son?

# Jeff Daniel Marion

## At the Wayside

Coming back in the fall dark
somehow I still expect to find
it the same: enter through
a screen door & there you are
lodged behind the counter, taking
arms against the last remaining
flies, swatter in hand
& eyes focused on the stock
market pages, dreaming of gold & Cadillacs.
Already at 14 that very day
our dreams had rounded to perfection:
the Yankees win again & Don Larsen
has pitched the perfect game:
now it is evening
Speedy turns full volume on the radio
replaying each strike, the blast of voices
beside the steaming black coffee on the counter
till he forgets the paper route that has mapped
35 years of his life.
It is the evening Buford Ray
leaves 5 games racked on the
pin-ball, leaps onto the counter
beside the radio, his hands cupped
to his mouth & puts Johnny Weissmuller
to shame in the best Tarzan yell
this side of the Roxy Theatre.
It is the evening Donnie Roy gooses
the waitress Evelyn Lee in the ribs,
frogs her arm & spins her out onto
the floor near the jukebox where already
Buford Ray has slugged the juke
as Kitty Wells' record whines,
the overhead fan whirls,

and the dancers spin & spin & spin with the world,
the sounds of feet, music, hands clapping
going out into the dark
searching the distances of stars & moon
until finally Mrs. Mapes looks up
over the stock market pages of her JOURNAL
& for the first time in nearly 15 years
a broad grin stretches her wrinkled cheeks
before she smacks her swatter on the cash
register and says, "Now boys."

And now I enter.
A face I've never seen before
rises, floats moon-like ion the mirror
behind the register.
Youth glistens in the hard light,
disguised only by a blond mustache:
"What for you, good buddy?"
"Change—change for a dollar," I say,
squinting into the light,
"just some change."
Past a still overhead fan,
past a door no longer screened,
I turn back to the waiting
dark, cold & starless.

# Julio Marzán

## Epitaph

Hours before my death,
Embarrassingly before the burial,
My flesh began to decay.
No strength could I spare explaining to friends

Why I stood up and walked to my grave.
Nor could I curse the cruelty of strangers
Amused by the crumbling ruins of a man
Leaving billows of ash in his trail.

No energy could I waste on bitterness.
All I had left, a skeleton of will,
Threaded my eroding limbs till my form,
Slowly propelled by the single thought,

Arrived whole. Here, on October 6, 1938,
Long my procession of strangers and friends,
Where now in the cool hollow of a box
Dust fills the darkness I became.


## Reverend Ewing Sends *Compasión* Magazine

Desirous of helping, desirous of seeing God
Bless me with a Cadillac's
Air suspension ride over the earth, Reverend Ewing's
Smile-illuminated face
Exhorts me to dream of the dollars, feel the peace
Oozing from people once wretched like me

Made blond with felicity when he,
Unhumanly fluent in God's own language,

Prayed in their names every night for a week;
Every piece in *Compasión* extols a miracle. So
I read eight black men finally find employment,
A million-dollar winner hits the lottery,
And the moving account of a widow
Deeply in love with that gentle companion
Solitude alone had not materialized.
And page after page Reverend Ewing is smiling.

Lighting up stadiums and the poor's rented halls,
Reverend Ewing is smiling;
White before kink, scars and rows of popped eyes,
Reverend Ewing is smiling;
Fluorescent with grace in his white working suit,
Teeth capped in doctored photographs,
Judeo-Christian and laissez faire,
Jingling the keys to the kingdom of Cadillac.

# Jim Wayne Miller

## In This Dream

In the dream we're crowded into the front seat
of a black '39 Chevrolet, my father, my grandfather, and I.
It is raining and the windshield wipers are whacking back
and forth, like a heartbeat, but I still can't see out
because the inside of the windshield is all fogged up.
We're wearing boots, plaid shirts, and denim jackets,
and over the jackets heavy overcoats, we're dressed for hunting.
I'm in the middle, my father on the passenger side, my grandfather
is driving and this is strange because he never learned
to drive. Not only is the windshield fogged, I am concerned
too because, jammed as we are, I have my head
over on my grandfather's chest and I don't think
his heart is beating, I think his heart has stopped.
I rub a little circle on the fogged windshield
and I can see the car is veering off the road toward
a row of fenceposts and I am trying to tell my father
I don't think my grandfather's heart is beating, I
don't think he's alive, and trying to get my grandfather's
heavy boot off the accelerator, him up off the wheel.
I see in the rearview mirror it's crowded in
the backseat too: there's a couple of my grandfather's
foxhunting buddies telling jokes, two foxhounds
whining eagerly, a muskrat with its foot caught
in a steeltrap keeps gnawing at its leg, there's a black bear
sitting with its nose pressed to a side window
the way my brother would sit watching the moon pace
along with the car and now they're all bouncing and pitching
in the backseat as we veer off the road and start clipping
fenceposts and I can't get my grandfather's foot
off the accelerator.

## Bird in the House

In a dogwood winter of grief he always turned
from fresh graves into another country.
Subtraction of lives from the land
altered fields, changed weather, shortened
seasons, made him—no longer a face reflected
in the cool springs of their eyes—
a sudden stranger to himself.

He turned always knowing their lives had bounded
the country he had known—the rounds and routines
of their days, little seasons, familiar weathers,
certain as rosebuds, fall apples or first frost,
their rooted lives great trees, his summer shade,
their stories on the porch at night: rain on the roof.

Like lines in the palms of their hands, paths
they made from house to barn to field got lost
in weeds and never came home. Fields and buildings
turned their backs on one another. A hill
eroded down to white limestone: flesh fallen from bones.

He always turned away with a heart fluttering
like a sparrow beating its wings at a window inside
the emptied house. Beyond a baffling hard
transparency: cedars, fenced fields, light, air,
country he came from.


## Skydiving

When I think of us seated in our separate days,
a hand under my breastbone tightens around a bar,
my seat tips back, rises, and my feet swing free,
as if I were riding a chair-lift in an amusement park.

We are strung out in five seats at fixed
distances from one another, dangling our feet

185

over treetops, over the heads of funny people
telescoped into themselves, whether thin or fat,

rising past several musics, past zebras and llamas
in their lots. Looking back at one another, we wave and clown.
One by one you turn ahead of me and, still climbing,
I touch my hand to yours as you pass, moving down.

When we are quiet in our separate rooms at night,
I think we are all skydivers falling through our
separate spaces. We float, lie prone in a circle.
Reaching out, we hold hands for a moment, then we're

off on our own currents, tumbling, backpedaling,
swimming or taking the sun in a playground
high over a brown yellow and green checkerboard
where roads run like lines in the palm of my hand.

It is pleasant and so still but we are falling
farther and farther apart through private corridors
of air. The earth grows under us, and begins
to be patches of ground the size of our shadows.

## Jungle Rot and Open Arms

*For a Vietnam Veteran brother, ex-prisoner*

Leavenworth
and jungle rot
brought him
back to us
brimming with hate
and disbelief
in love or
sympathy.

his johnnywalker red
eyes
tore at my words
shred my flesh
made naked my
emptiness.

my anger
for the enemy heads
of state
boiled to nothing
            nothing
in the wake
of his rage

jungle rot
had sucked his bones
his skin fell
like the monsoon
his brain
in a cast in Leavenworth.

In the midst
of genocide

**187**

he fell in love
in Vietnam.

> "Her hair was
> long and dark—like yours"
>             he said
> "her eyes held the
> sixth moon
> and when she smiled
> the sky opened
> and I fell through.
>
> I would crawl
> in the tall grasses
> to her village
>
> and sleep the war
> away with her
> like a child on my thighs
>
> I did not know
> of the raid
>
> and woke
>
> with her arm
> still clasping mine
>
> I could not find
> the rest of her
>
> so I buried her arm
> and marked my grave."

We sat in a silence
that mocks fools
that lifts us to the final language.

his breath sapped by B-52's
his eyes blinded by the blood of children

his hands bound to bayonets
his soul buried in a shallow grave

i stood amidst
his wreckage
and wept for myself.

so where is my
*political education?* my
*rhetoric answers* to everything? my
*theory in practice?* my
*intensification of life in art?*

words
are
like
the stone,
the gravemarker
over an arm
in Vietnam.

## What Matters

The things that matter
you ask, where is love?
The poem
soft as linen
dried by the sun?
words of comfort
like puffed pillows
yellow flowers
with velvet petals?
Where is serenity,
cherry blossoms arranged,
the quaint ceremony of tea?
Images metaphysically deep
spoken in Japanese,

preferably seventeen syllables
of
persimmons or new
plums or snow covered bridges
or red flow of leaves?
What matters
the trickling clarity of
water
each day, not fearing thirst.
        I love you
when persimmons sweat
shining in a sand gray bowl,
        Mama
hiding pennies
under floor boards
with flour, saltine crackers,
balls of used aluminum foil,
string, coupons and water jars
secreted for that day.
That day
when all would be taken
and packing
must be quick again.
        I love you
when snow covers the bridge
curved over ice white water
        Grandfather
killing my cat
who ripped open his hens,
sucking their eggs.
His eyes, half closed
behind steel rims,
cigarette holder
clenched in his teeth,
as he fondled the rock.
Before I could cry
or plead,
my cat, writhing
with skull crushed.
He captured a rabbit,
gave it to me
and warned

we would eat in winter
as soon as I began to love her.

    I love you
when plums burst like new moons,
crescents on their black boughs
    my husband
whose dark hands
embrace the wilted shoulders
of the wretched,
winos with wracked eyes,
and welfare mothers cleaning cockroaches
from the lips of their children.
His words
like spoons, nourishing.
    I love you
when leaves flow in crimson,
orange, yellow, sepia waves
    my daughter
who weeps for each dead
seal, murdered tiger,
cat's corpse, endangered species
of condor and chinese panda,
crusading against gamesmen
and trophy hunters.
    What matters,
Breath
for the shipwrecked, drowning.
    What matters
amidst the dread of nuclear winter,
Chernobyl's catastrophe, Three Mile Island,
Nevada's test veterans, terrorism,
the massacred in Port Elizabeth, the
wounded of Central America, genocide of drugs,
AIDS, toxic waste, Atlanta's missing
and mutilated, hunger, mistaken identities,
murder in the streets.
    A love poem?

    Clear water passing    (5)
    our mouths unafraid to breathe,    (7)
    and to speak freely.    (5)

**191**

# Reversals

*For Layne*

I find myself
now, sending
you words on yellow paper
to share my void,
the fears, the small complaints
that make hairline
wrinkles around my mouth.
I remember
when we searched
as children
in the fields,
in the abandoned
fallen chick houses,
I for insects
to pin my collection,
my insects, neatly pinned
guarded against you,
in the convent of my room.
Your search
for the streak of gold
in rocks,
black little stones,
joyful, envied by me.
You seemed so fearless
of loss or failure.
A stone cast aside,
worthless, quickly forgotten,
while I
as if to gather small, irreplaceable
bits of myself,
would stockpile
broken wings,
dismembered limbs
and carefully add
to my collection.
My brother,
I did not know

your manhood would not consume
my barren room,
impaled with dead butterflies.
Nor that your capacity
for joy, your ease
with life
could streak gold
on this small stone,
my heart.

# James Masao Mitsui

## Destination: Tule Lake Relocation Center, May 20, 1942

She had raised the window
higher

than her head; then
paused

to life wire spectacles,
wiping

sight back with a wrinkled
hand-

kerchief. She wanted to watch
the old

place until the train's passing
erased

the tarpaper walls and tin roof;
she had

been able to carry away
so little.

The finger of her left
hand

worried two strings
attached

to a baggage tag
flapping

from her
lapel.

# Allowance

I am ten.
My mother sits in a black
rocking chair in the parlor
and tells stories of a country school
surrounded by ricefields
and no roads.

I stand in the kerosene light
behind her,
earning my allowance.
A penny
for each white hair I pull.

# The East Watch House

"Yesterday is a cloud of steam and the train is out of sight."

Jill Ruthruff

I sneak outside in the thick snow
of the night.

I sneak outside,
the sky hangs like a canopy
and I step into my father's bootprints
that lead beyond the circle
of our porchlight.

Father inches into the silence
down the tracks,
his lantern bouncing
as it wavers out of sight.
Snow falls in curtains
and I wonder if I love him.

Tomorrow he will tell me
about the overtime,
what he took to eat
and how he kept warm.

195

I turn back to the dim lights
of the house. I will know he is all right
if the trains keep running through town.


## During a Fit of Positive Thinking even as Snow Threatens Our February Spring and Channel 5 Says It's 82° in Havana

> *"Hearts will not be practical until they are made unbreakable."*
>
> The Wizard of Oz

Walking the garbage out to the dumpster,
I don't care that the moon is sharp, not yellow.

This time I'm leaving the tight stomach and 3 A.M.
ceiling to those monster movies and first divorces.

On my desk I keep a rock picked up on Dungeness Spit.
Its heavy marble keeps books propped open

and its whiteness reminds me of official London.
Do people take honeymoons just for the travel?

We never catch up to every answer. A Mason jar
holds five crimson tulips spreading

like June on a Shogi board
next to my work. Twenty-two degrees

and I don't even feel like sighing.
Music is such a fine cover.

I have a confession: today I witnessed
a student from the Philippines

interrupt work on a paper
to meditate, palms

touching like Gandhi,
and I was proud to be her teacher.

# José Montoya

## Rough Time in th' Barrio

It was not th' first time—
Budgetary constraints
Had occurred before
In th' early seventies
I remember.

So when I mentioned
The Barrio Art Program
Monies had been frozen
The Ancianos were
Very understanding.

They told me not to worry
That things would get
Better and one or
Two of th' feisty Seniors
Suggested we make a
Protest at City Hall, some
One yelled out—it's the college,
Not the city!
We all laughed and the fact
We hadn't gotten yarn
Was forgotten and we
Steeped ourselves in
Other artsy craftsy
Projects that night

At the end of class
Luisita came up to me
Grabbed my shoulder
Gently as I was leaving
And looked around and
Coyly but very assuredly

Handed me a brown bag
With a huge slab of
Give-away cheeze and
Two two-pound slabs
Of butter and told
Me not to worry

". . . take this to your familia
And don't you worry Senor
Professor—todo saldra bien!"

Holding back a gasp I hurried out.
I sat in my pick-up
And cried for a short,
Guilty, joyous, embarrassing
Instant and quickly glanced
Around hoping the Barrio
Wasn't watching my truck

Tough time in th' barrio
In this decade of the Hispanic—
Y la calma Chicano endures.

# Cherríe Moraga

## Poema como valentín (or a San Francisco Love Poem)

An artist friend once
showed me how to see
color as a black & white phenomenon.

Look.
See that broad-faced glistening
leaf? Look.
See where it is white, a light
magnet to the sun?
Look.
See where it is black?

The eye narrows
into a core
pin point focus
of what was never green, really
only light condensing
into dark.

.    .    .

You could paint a portrait
this way, seeing
from black to white.

Her mouth would still be rose
and round, but less tired
of explaining itself
and as I pressed mine to it
it could remember no mouth
evenly vaguely reminiscent, no mouth
with this particular blend of wet

and warm in the darkest
and fullest part

that sustains me
while all the world of this city
weeps

under a blanket
of intercepted
light.

# Rosario Morales

## Old

### Una

My mother at thirty was as luminous as the Puerto Rican dawn over the cream sand beaches curving in and out and around the island. She was like the moist fruit of the mango, like the fronds of the royal palm in the wind. And I knew thirty was what I was going to be when I lost the skeleton I wore, and when I grew old, grew beautiful and free.

### Dos

Skin
practicing to be old—
lining up, squaring off:
tracings
etchings
bas relief.

Look!
Over the blue
creek beds of my veins,
how the wrinkling
ripples sparkle
in the sun.

### Tres

Que clase de vieja will I be when I knew none, grew up in New York City when El Barrio was young like me and grandmothers grew in Puerto Rico, when grandmothers were kept fresh in boxes of pictures under the bed and became flesh only the summer I was going to be ten. We took a long sickening boat ride of a week to the magical landscape of Naranjito and on its one street I became "¡Mira! la hija de Lola, la de Mercedes." Abuela Mercedes was just like her photograph: large cotton-wrapped, her breasts squared off onto her middle, hammocks of face dripping onto her chin, cushions of her melting into the brown floorboards. She smelled like maduros frying. And while the music from the jukebox across the street flies about her shoulders, crashes into the hibiscus bush, the guayaba, and as she stands imperturbable, solid, only her flesh giving way, I am comforted and afraid.

I cannot turn to my other grandmother. Abuela Rosario sat small, sat thin, sat straight and hard in a hard chair, knobbed hands on a knobbed stick. She beat one girl and ten boys into adulthood, and my father beat me, and I beat my babies and bit my hands and looked for knobs.

## Cuatro

Crow's wings not feet—pinions
anchored to my eyes.
They spread in flight only
when I smile.
I smile.

## Cinco

She warned me as she added sugar to the roasting coffee beans to blacken the brew, "Don't go out into the damp air, the cool night, after a day tostando café in an open pan over a hot fire, porque te va' a pa'mar." She said, "¡Cuidao, o te va' a pa'mar!" And she meant that the moment I hit the evening chill my warm skin would shrivel and wrinkle and ruck, a surrealer Rip Van Winkle. Only a moment would go by and I'd be old, old, older than old Doña Cornelia herself who always carefully wrapped a towel around her head and shoulders like a shawl before she left her burnt-sugar brown kitchen and stepped out beneath the banana leaves hiding the stars.

## Seis

Maga was Jane's mother, my best friend's mother, was Alabama born, high-born, white as her hair, and even after twenty years in Puerto Rico couldn't speak Spanish and her a communist like her red-haired daughter, like her Puerto Rican son-in-law, like me.

I wanted to be like her when I grew old, I wanted the freedom to say what I liked, when I liked, to whom I like. I wanted to pour Lapsang Souchong out of a china teapot into the endless afternoon and tell others what to do and how to do it. I wanted what I thought it felt like, sitting tall and high-handed, hair cut short and crisp, straight spine keeping the cops from stepping through the door to take her son-in-law César away, lean slacks bending, lean hands reaching to grasp the garden weeds and smack the roots free of soil, grasping too, at her daughter's home, her son, her time. And when Jane died, she reached for mine.

I couldn't give you that! But oh, Maga, will I sit as you sat, lone-handed, sipping tepid tea into the night?

### Siete

Stop!
I don't want my scalp
        shining through a few thin hairs.
Don't want my neck skin to hang—
        neglected cobweb—in the corner of my chin.

Stop!     at ruckling ruches of skin
          at soft sags,
               bags of tongue tickling breast and belly,
          at my carved face.

No further.
Stop.

### Ocho

no quiero morir

# Thylias Moss

## Lessons from a Mirror

Snow White was nude at her wedding, she's so white
the gown seemed to disappear when she put it on.

Put me beside her and the proximity is good
for a study of chiaroscuro, not much else.

Her name aggravates me most, as if I need to be told
what's white and what isn't.

Judging strictly by appearance there's a future for me
at her heels, a shadowy protege she acknowledges only

at certain times of day. Is it fair for me to live
that way, unable to get off the ground?

Turning the tables isn't fair unless they keep turning.
Then there's the danger of Russian roulette

and my disadvantage: nothing falls from the sky
to name me.

I am empty space where the tooth was, that my tongue
rushes to fill because I can't stand vacancies.

And it's not enough. The penis just fills another
gap. And it's not enough.

When you look at me,
know that more than white is missing.

# More Lessons from a Mirror

In Alice's reversed world
she must have wondered why they called her
nigger
when she knew
her face was white as flour
having seen it in a mirror.

Three boys climbed on top of a box and jumped,
hammering nails into the head of the boy inside.
I live with them on the wrong side of the mirror.
And though I read of Alice's successful journey
I had also read how all men are equal
at the moment of creation only.

There's something wrong with the mirrors
in my eyes.
Sometimes death rows are pews in a church.
Laundry drying in the sun is inhabited
by men dangling from live wires.
Bonneted women won't churn much butter
plunging handles into detonators.

Watching the movie *Pinky* I didn't share the grief
of a white woman portraying a black woman
pretending to be a white woman.
I could only see Jean Crain's face lost
in Ethel Water's dark bosom.

Then I realized
there's no better grave.

# David Mura

## The Natives

Several months after we lost our way,
they began to appear, their quiet eyes
assuring us, their small painted legs
scurrying beside us. By then our radio
had been gutted by fungus, our captain's cheek
stunned by a single bullet; our ammo vanished
the first night we discovered our maps were useless,
our compasses a lie. (The sun and stars
seemed to reel above us.) The second week
forced us on snakes, monkeys, lizards, and toads;
we ate then raw over wet smoking fires.
Waking one morning we found a river boat
loaded with bodies hanging in trees
like an ox on a sling, marking the stages
of flood. One of us thought he heard the whirr
of a chopper, but it was only the monsoon
drumming the leaves, soaking our skin so damp
you felt you could peel it back to scratch
the bones of your ankle. Gradually our names
fell from our mouths, never heard again.
Nights, faces glowing, we told stories of wolves,
and the jungle seemed colder, more a home.

And then we glimpsed them, like ghosts of children
darting through the trees, the curtain of rain;
we told each other nothing, hoping they'd vanish.
But one evening the leaves parted. Slowly
they emerged and took our hands, their striped
faces dripping, looking up in wonder
at our grizzled cheeks. Stumbling like gods
without powers, we carried on our backs
what they could not carry, the rusted grenades,
the ammoless rifles, barrels clotted with flies.
They waited years before they brought us

206

to their village, led us in circles till
time disappeared. Now, stone still, our feet
tangled with vines, we stand by their doorway
like soft-eyed virgins in the drilling rain:
the hair on our shoulders dangles and shines.


## Grandfather and Grandmother in Love

Now I will ask for one true word beyond
betrayal, that creaks and buoys like the bedsprings
used by the bodies that begot the bodies that begot me.
Now I will think of the moon bluing the white
sheets soaked in sweat, that heard him whisper
haiku of clover, azaleas, the cry of the cuckoo;
complaints of moles and beetles,
blight and bad debts, as the *biwa's* spirit
bubbled up between them, its song quavering.
Now I take this word and crack it, like a seed
between the teeth, spit it out into the world,
and let it seek the loam that nourished his greenhouse
roses, sputtering petals of chrysanthemum:
let it leave the sweet taste of *teriyaki*,
and a grain of rice lodges in my molars,
and the faint breath of *sake*, hot in the nostrils.
Now the drifting before writhing, now Buddha
stand back, now he bumps beside her,
*otoo-san*, *okaa-san*, calling each other.
Now there reverberates the *ran* of lovers,
and the bud of the past has burst through
into the other world,
where she, teasing, pushes him away, swats
his hand, like a pesky, tickling fly,
and then turns to his face that cries out
laughing, and he is hauling her in, trawling
the caverns of her flesh, gathering gift
after gift from a sea that seems endless,
depths a boy dreams of, where dolphins
and fluorescent fins and fish with wings
suddenly spill their glittering scales

before him, and he, who was always baffled by beauty,
lets slip the net and dives under, and the night
washes over them, slipping from sight,
just the soft shushing of waves, drifting ground
swells, echoing the knocking tide of morning.


## Nantucket Honeymoon

It's easy for bees to build their combs of honey, or for apples to drop, their
    light absorbed,
but once only the dazzle and delirium of bodies tumbling on top of me
could sing the tirade taking my life—I was white, yes, like the bodies I
    claimed—
And when I wanted to say it wasn't my nature, my color, my will failed. I
    could not

stop . . . Since then, since then, I've become someone I never expected.
At times I'd like to think it some great act of character or even a miracle
God was preparing, long before I finally said: I give. *No mas.* Can't take it
    anymore.
But no, it wasn't like that. You were entering med school, I felt threatened,

I'd been reading Menniger's *Man Against Himself,* saw myself too often
in its pages. And looking at friends, recent marriages, soon-to-be babies,
I think it was probably just as much the times, just growing up. That
and learning—how else can I say it?—to love my own sweet skin.

And now?—On this island of wild mustard, mist and heather, herring gulls
careening in the salty, rackety Madaket wind, we walk the beach, party
to the triumph of the palpable and small—A conch in your palm, my palm
on your shoulder, a fork you hold up, its lemony halibut, mousse or
    pate . . .

Later, from our bed, I can see the steeple and its lights, the full moon; your
    head
a familiar book, bobbing on my chest. (How far I feel from that Asian
    island.)
Years away our grandchildren will come here saying, *This room is where I
began.*

And returning to Boston, Paris or Portland, won't know how bewildered I
    was,

how alone. They'll think I felt American. I was always at home.


## Lost in the Philippines


### 1 Northern Luzon: A Dream

Bound for the terraced
rice fields of Banaue, stranded,
no jeepney till dawn,
in a browned-out mountain town,
I matched beers with two civil guards:
as their faces floated into
blackness, as the night crept in,
I saw a look ancient, Indian,
and thought I was lost in the Andes
and would never get back. I
got back, and slept that night
in Enrique's house, listened
to his mother-in-law complain
about no respect for authority,
about human rights, and when I
woke with two hands smothering
my mouth, I knew I would die
like a dog, choking and squealing, robbed
for my weakness and American sins.
But it was only the blueness of a
cock's crow, the hot glistening
touch of my wacky paranoia,
and beneath a huge portrait of
Ferdinand and Imelda, I fell back to
sleep, recalling your face, rippling
down my body, shuddering in
affection, a pure white dream.

## 2 Visions of Dharma

Once in a cold green office, amid a cluster of photos
—river, cane fields, a child of Negros, the bloated body—
a woman's cigarette burned to a long finger of ash,
and when the night and neon of Tokyo flooded the window,
I, like a fool, wondered why her taut, dark face still bloomed
with a stream of rage, the hours and years of her island,
till she was no longer young, no longer beautiful,
and the century was still closing like a damp, dark wound.

Once, past the rusted tin shacks of squatters, past children
waving and wading waist high in monsoon sewage,
I came to the great trash heaps of Manila, smoking in the rain
(there scavengers pick their living three shifts a day).
Near evening, a girl laughed, stepped from a doorway, sporting
a Madonna t-shirt, a plastic gold chair. Fresh from street craps
and sniffing glue, using the five Japanese words she possessed,
she tugged my arm. I blushed, stammered, hurried away.

Today, wandering past jade trees, Kyoto's white gardens,
I found schoolchildren in uniforms and yellow caps
shouting to my wife, *Haroo! haroo!* After kimonos embroidered
with lilies, pearl scabbards and samurai blades, castles
with peacocks, near the golden temple that vanished
in seething flames, a hill of granite graves, I grew tired
of beauty, my endless wandering, and felt my self blur:
In the late, soft burred sunlight, suddenly hoardes

of Asians, gooks, mongols, slant-eyed slopes; coolies
and kimonos, *ao dais* and brabble brown Filipinos,
came tumbling, laughing and chanting, tearing to tatters
my white boy dreams. Out of breath and blacking out,
I saw my soul, crouched, cramped in the womb, hearing Buddha
mumble this blessing or curse—"Obey and rebel in equal
proportion, despise, covet, flesh/spirit, rich/poor, yellow/white"—
and this, this angry whisper—"*Bakka*. Get on with your life!"

210

# Duane Niatum

## No One Remembers the Village of White Fir

### I

As a child of cedar, hemlock, and the sea,
I often slept under totem and star,
hanging from the black lids
of a bat's closed eyes to muffle my soul
from the drone of my mother's wrath.

Time formed itself with Elwah rhymes,
the rainbow river of my ancestors,
whose art was fishing, hunting,
basket weaving, dance, and occasionally war.
The wind then clacked like a bone rattle,
shaking alpine meters from the dark.
Salmon swam the rapid dreams
of those children playing
with the bluejay and chipmunk.
And when my grandfather died in my youth,
I sealed up cave after cave.

### II

Dancing to the eagle's nest, my blood soared.
On hearing the river in the morning,
I followed its heartbeat to the sky,
reached the snow tip of Memp-ch-ton,
the white wing of its summit,
where wild rose and lupine
rooted to the breaks in stone.

On some days I ran through a childhood
of a dozen myths, saw the fruit

on the chokeberry tree ripen
in the light of Black Cherries Moon.
I plucked those memories for my escape
from the wreckage of scars.

### III

I crawled deeper into the cave,
inching my way from the nightmare.
I was furless, a bear clawing my way,
out of the hissing, howling blizzard.
Seatco chased me to the edge of my cries;
Raven tossed me into skunk's arms.
My grandfather who appeared
in the blackwinged passage sadly
shook his head, shamed by my fear,
but not my failure. Grandfather,
you and Great Uncle and your father were
the only men I have known: your spirits
have been my shield. Someday, may
I face the storm with your courage,
offer your songs to the children
and the nameless poor?

### IV

Figures woven into the baskets' sides
work quietly through the morning;
and the women who collected the grass
and bark for weaving are always the first
to see the sun touch the river.
Hoping to live out his vision,
an elder watches the wrens eating berries,
makes promises to the moon one last night.

### V

Spinning on the colors of the meadow,
the earth covers up her tracks
with a celebration of acorn and warm winds.

The women picking roots tease the children.
Yet today the old paths are harder
to find like the eagle, deer, the fern pickers.
And the eroding forest barely draws
the stranger into the clearing,
the red-bone center of sunrise.


## VI


Watching for the shifts in the orange fire,
I seek the glow of a cedar cone in ash,
to burn in the city, until the face
of O-le-man smiles before vanishing
in the rainbow. Never quite as constant
as the moon, I speak to the bats again—
stop when Trickster calls

    "Niatum!    Niatum!"


## Spider


Stop, friends, spin with me past
the morning rain, the morning rain.
Touch the yellow, orange, and green threads—
feel the thunder that passed my house!

And if by chance, by accidental dance,
we meet where the meadow's a violet ledge,
don't be frightened by my traces,
they were woven to delight the sun.

    There are things about us
    too beautiful to lose;
    our many-colored song
    not even the Raven knows.

# Dream of the Burning Longhouse

Spinning away from the center,
lost to the flames, the old ones
break down to shadow and ash.
Without their songs of growing
brittle as the hemlocks,
will I be banished from my blood's country?
Has my heart thrown the drum to the earth?
My spirit forgotten its song to the mountains?
Oh my body, are you telling our story to the cave?

# Harold Norse

## To Walt and Hart

The brown book stashed
beside the spear, teak bow
unstrung from Africa, form
small defense against the world's hard core
of twisted words and deeds. The book
with messages of trucks and wharves,
rhythms and coffee smells
of trade on rotting piers, of men
on lone patrol for alcohol, kisses, gleam
of bellies—your book, Crane,
whose gashed spine counts the decades as
ringed trunks of oak reveal
the years—I've
tended, nurtured it, ripe with metaphor,
from youth's first worship
"past my utmost year." Year of post mortem?
Hart, in Walt's hand yours—my hand
in both, my heart crossing
the river—Charon's Styx?
Walt's Brooklyn ferry? or Brooklyn Bridge?
Sacred journey under the choiring steel. Thence
to eternity—*quo vadis?*—man and boy,
the voyage done. Now
ended? Cutty Sarked? Clipped dreams.
From the *Orizaba* deck (I was fifteen) you leapt.
Later, in your room, two years later, I wept.
My gaze rose from your window rapt
with awe, your myth before my eyes—like Keats's hair
I fingered that year in Morgan's library,
curled under my touch—wisp of time
writ in water . . . you
cut syllables in the song
of the River that is East—I caught
the tune, beneath the cabled spires, harped
the selfsame theme . . . the *Bridge!*

## The Canaries in Uncle Arthur's Basement

In the white house in Rutherford
the ancient upright piano never worked
and the icy kitchen smell of Spic 'n Span.
Aunt Lizzie's pumpkin pie turned out green
and no one ate it but me and I did
because it was the green of the back porch.
That was the Thanksgiving it rained and I first thought
of rain as tears, because Aunt Lizzie was in tears
because Arthur came home from the soccer game drunk
and because he missed dinner, brought a potted plant
for each female relative, and walked around the table
kissing each one as Lizzie said "Arthur, you
fool, you fool," the tears running down her cheeks as
Arthur's knobby knees wobbled in his referee's
shorts, and his black-striped filthy shirt wet from the rain
looked like a convict's. What did I know?
I thought it meant something. I thought
no one would ever be happy again. I thought
if I were Uncle Arthur I'd never again
come out from the dark basement where he raised canaries,
the cages wrapped in covers Aunt Lizzie sewed,
and where, once, when I was very small and because Uncle Arthur
loved me or loved his skill or both he slowly removed the cover
from a cage and a brilliant gold bird burst into song.

## Having Built the Coop

*"For centuries I have been forced to sleepwalk on these roads of decay."*

d. A. Levy, "The North American Book of the Dead"

I put the chickens in and they swivel
their necks, tentative, suspicious,
their merciless unblinking eyes

reminders that they descended
from reptiles, though these are loveable
as they coo and cluck and their behinds
wiggle as they settle down to turn
the tiny compound into a mud flat
and then don't even try to escape,
though the grass they love is growing
luxuriantly a few inches beyond
the woven wire fence, because the coop
is home and from my point of view
I want their eggs in one place
even though it's the nature of chickens
insofar as one can talk about "nature"
to be pecking through a broad universe
of an acre or more, and I suppose
the moral, if there is a "moral,"
is what levy said: it's all illusion,
but you may as well follow your own
as the illusions of others—though the chickens
don't care, the chickens cackle over some
culled spinach they adore and a handful
of cracked corn and cluck "this is
the best place in the world" though
of course they haven't been to any other
because they're in a cage but that's ok,
they don't live too long and they're
never going to read Thucydides or
hit many good restaurants, they
are there to work, and it amazes me
how intelligent levy was for someone
who died at 23 but still understood
that "everyone pays their dues
& no one's gettin' the product"
though that was twenty years back
and none of the chickens are complaining
this June as the invisible cicadas sing
*derrida . derrida . derrida*

# Simon Ortiz

## Canyon de Chelly

Lie on your back on stone,
the stone carved to fit
the shape of yourself.
Who made it like this,
knowing that I would be along
in a million years and look
at the sky being blue forever?

My son is near me. He sits
and turns on his butt
and crawls over to stones,
picks one up and holds it,
and then puts it into his mouth.
The taste of stone.
What is it but stone,
the earth in your mouth.
You, son, are tasting forever.

We walk to the edge of cliff
and look down into the canyon.
On this side, we cannot see
the bottom cliffedge but looking
further out, we see fields,
sand furrows, cottonwoods.
In winter, they are softly gray.
The cliffs' shadows are distant,
hundreds of feet below;
we cannot see our own shadows.
The wind moves softly into us.
My son laughs with the wind;
he gasps and laughs.

We find gray root, old wood,
so old, with curious twists

in it, curving back into curves,
juniper, piñon, or something
with hard, red berries in spring.
You taste them, and they are sweet
and bitter, the berries a delicacy
for bluejays. The plant rooted
fragilely into a sandy place
by a canyon wall, the sun bathing
shiny, pointed leaves.

My son touches the root carefully,
aware of its ancient quality.
He lays his soft, small fingers on it
and looks at me for information.
I tell him: wood, an old root,
and around it, the earth, ourselves.


## Watching Salmon Jump

It was you:
I could have crawled
between mountains—
that is where seeds are possible—
and touched the soft significance
of roots of birth and the smell of newborn fish

       and

know how it is
leaping into rock
so that our children may survive.

# Raymond R. Patterson

## Twenty-Six Ways of Looking at a Blackman

*For Boydie & Ama*

### I

On the road we met a blackman,
But no one else.

### II

Dreams are reunions. Who has not
On occasion entertained the presence
Of a blackman?

### III

From brown paper bags
A blackman fills the vacancies of morning
With orange speculations.

### IV

Always I hope to find
The blackman I know,
Or one who knows him.

### V

Devouring earthly possessions
Is one of a blackman's excesses.
Exaggerating their transiency
Is another.

## VI

Even this shadow has weight.
A cool heaviness.
Call it a blackman's ghost.

## VII

The possibilities of color
Were choices made by the eye
Looking inward.
The possibilities of rhythms
For a blackman are predetermined.

## VIII

When it had all been unravelled,
The blackman found that it had been
Entirely woven of black thread.

## IX

Children who loved him
Hid him from the world
By pretending he was a blackman.

## X

The fingerprints of a blackman
Were on her pillow. Or was it
Her luminous tears?
. . . An absence, or a presence?
Only when it was darker
Would she know.

## XI

The blackman dipped water
From a well.

221

And when the well dried,
He dipped cool blackness.


## XII

We are told that the seeds
Of rainbows are not unlike
A blackman's tear.


## XIII

What is more beautiful than black flowers,
Or blackmen in fields
Gathering them?
. . . The bride, or the wedding?


## XIV

When it was finished,
Some of the carvers of Destiny
Would sigh in relief,
But the blackman would sigh in intaglio,
Having shed vain illusions in mastering the stone.


## XV

Affirmation of negatives:
A blackman trembles
That his thoughts run toward darkness.


## XVI

The odor of a blackman derives
No less from the sweat of his apotheosis,
Than emanation of crushed apples
He carries in his arms.

## XVII

If I could imagine the shaping of Fate,
I would think of blackmen
Handling the sun.

## XVIII

Is it harvest time in the brown fields,
Or is it just a black man
Singing?

## XIX

There is the sorrow of blackmen
Lost in cities. But who can conceive
Of cities lost in a blackman?

## XX

A small boy lifts a seashell
To his listening ear.
It is the blackman again,
Whispering his sagas of drowned sailors.

## XXI

At the cradle of Justice were found
Three gifts: a pair of scales, a sword,
And a simple cloth. But the Magi had departed.
Several who were with us agreed
One of the givers must have been
A blackman.

## XXII

As vines grow towards light,
So roots grow towards darkness.

223

Back and forth a blackman goes,
Gathering the harvest.


## XXIII

By moonlight
We tossed our pebbles into the lake
And marveled
At the beauty of concentric sorrows.
You thought it was like the troubled heart
Of a blackman,
Because of the dancing light.


## XXIV

As the time of our leave taking drew near,
The blackman blessed each of us
By pronouncing the names of his children.


## XXV

As I remember it,
The only unicorn in the park
Belonged to a blackman
Who went about collecting bits
And torn scraps of afternoons.


## XXVI

At the center of Being
Said the blackman,
All is tangential.
Even this laughter, even your tears.

# Jean Pedrick

## Redlight

*Now there are three kinds of martyrdom which are accounted as a Cross to a man, white martyrdom, green martyrdom, and red martyrdom. White martyrdom consists in a man's abandoning everything he loves for God's sake. . . . Green martyrdom consists in this, that by means of fasting and labour he frees himself from his evil desires; or suffers toil in penance and repentance. Red martyrdom consists in the endurance of a Cross or death for Christ's sake.*

From a Celtic homily, 7th century

It's a tight prison—marriage,
and in green martyrdom alert all ears
to catch one sugar thread of faraway music
like the city tree that roots in pavement,
that stinks, in May, of its thick slather
set to get all the wind can bring,
stinks, in fact, like a mammal
with the similar problem. . . .

*Then why not go?* A youthful question
and legitimate. And can recite my friends
known by their feats, the names began
to shine the day they threw the dishes,
duffels and kids and artworks in the car
and put their foot down and went . . .

I'd have done it. My kids and yours
I'd have thrown in the car and we'd
have done well, we two, with our ancient
skills, wherever the wheel came off . . .

But I see you even now, standing—
not lying down as the dead should do—
standing there rooted in God, the weight
of the tablets of Moses in your pockets.

## Carefully

Carefully circumventing
every elephant trap—
dead brush is not live bramble;
carefully climbing each tree
by whippy, sapful stirrups,
never the clean black rungs
of deadwood; carefully sailing
home free and in time for supper
from all forbidden islets—
the placement of the first foot
in very small boats is everything:

I, carefully, always, of my own
volition, at every *crise* and turning
of my life, made every destined,
preconditioned, nonpreventable
wily and wilful choice like a killer
log on the flood. I chose you.


## The Inlet

I came to a shore. And you were there,
my perished love, just as in mankind's
fondest expectation, on the other side.

A short pull in a small skiff. But
as I near the edge I see it's not a river—
it is an inlet. Just keep walking
and I'll presently be where you are.

       He is walking along the quay
       in an adriatic light.
       He is wearing an open shirt.
       How fine he looks!    How rested!

226

If I break and run,
if I give a loud call: "Halloo!"
if you turn and wave . . .

       A wash of houses, rose-petal, ivory,
       their eyes deep-set.    Clusters
       of piney herb in flower.    One tree
       yearning outward over water
       catching flights of fishes
       in the reflection of its arms.

# Robert Peters

## Song for a Son

My son's image
was painted on sand.

The wind from off the lake
bears me no news of him,
nor of his impression.

Was it arrogance to think
I could hold his features?

I had set them in memory,
fashioned cameos for the
mind, had seen that face at will,
in various attitudes, transforming
me—when he was alive.

But I am blind!
Unable to create a brow,
a lash, the hollow down
the back of the neck,
the throat!

Look.
Those trees hold nothing
in their branches. Those rushes
by the lake, so rife with
blackbirds, hold nothing:

     Mist faces,
     faces in shrouds,
     faces in clouds . . .

Water has worn the cameos down

# Miscarriage

My mother bathes alone—
the metal tub, the kettle
of hot water, on a strip
of carpet, in her room.

She has lost another child.
Dad buries it under the birches
behind the well.

God is on her side.
She didn't want the child.
He listened to her when she cried.
He opened a fresh wound wide
in His eternal side.
The baby slipped in and hid there
when he died.

# The Sow's Head

The day was like pewter.
The gray lake a coat
open at the throat. The border
of trees-frayed mantle collar,
hairs, evergreen. The sky dun.
Chilling breeze. Hem of winter.

I passed the iodine-colored brook
hard waters open
the weight of the sow's head
an ache from shoulder to waist,
the crook of my elbow numb.
Juices seeping through
the wrapping paper.

I was wrong to take it.
There were meals in it.

I would, dad said, assist
with slaughter, scrape off
hair, gather blood.
I would be whipped for
thieving from the dogs.

I crossed ice
which shivered, shone.
No heads below, none;
nor groans—only water, deep,
and the mud beds of frogs asleep;
not a bush quivered,
not a stone. Snow.

Old snow had formed
hard swirls      bone
and planes with
windwhipped ridges
for walking upon;
and beneath, in the deep,
bass quiet, perch whirling
fins, bluegills, sunfish,
dim-eyed soaking heat.
Mud would be soft down there,
rich, tan, deeper than a man:
silt of leeches, leaves
tumbling in from trees,
loon feces, mulch-thick
mudquick, and lignite forming,
cells rumbling, rifts.

I knelt, chopped through
layers of ice until
water, pus, spilled up
choking the wound. I widened
the gash. Tchick! Tchick!
chips of ice flew.
Water blew from the hole,

the well, a whale, expired.
My knees were stuck to the ice.

I unwrapped the paper.
The head appeared
shorn of its beard.
Its ears stood up, the snout
with its Tinker Toy holes
held blood. Its eyes were shut.
There was grain on its mouth.

It sat on the snow
as though it lived below,
leviathan come for air
limbs and hulk
dumb to my presence there.

I raised the sow's head
by its ears. I held it
over the hole, let it go,
watched it sink, a glimmer
of pink, a wink of a match
an eyelid . . .

A bone in my side beat.

# Felice Picano

## Three Men Speak to Me

### i. Tony

That summer we rode giant white frisbees
over the surf, gliding an eighth of an inch
over sand, seventy-five feet at a slide—
we were like gods of the sea. Shaun moved
to the West Coast for good, while Kelly bought
yards of white muslin to hang in the house.
At night it was lighted like the inside
of a skull. White muslin, white pillows, white
everything! It was the summer of, the
year of, the decade-return of designed
China-white! I wondered what my hair
would look like gone white . . . When it happened
Peter was gone, Vinnie was sick. I only
needed six days—never knew what hit me.

### ii. David

They would stand outside the shop on Bleecker
Street and look in at me while I checked
bills of lading. Some waved. Few came in. It
was summer again but my breezy gray
*blouson* was long sleeved to cover the spots.
Bad for business: not that I cared. Only
I counted. Every day I would stare into
scores of brass and silver-gilt mirrors
around me for sale, from France, "the real stuff"
George said, and see myself shrink, age by
the hour. Just two years before I'd been a star
in a French porno flick about jaded New
York—the toast of Paree! If you care to ask

232

I'd tell you how bitter it tasted. Not
my life, which I loved, not the ups, fists,
dicks that I'd spun on, but this kind of end.
I'd never asked for anything special, had I?
Lived on almost nothing. Never had lover.
Never made trouble . . . I especially
hated it when my anus began to cave in.
I should have gone to live in France in 'Sixty-
Eight, like I'd planned to.


### iii. Sheldon

Writing a will was the difficult part—
asking next-door neighbors to witness.
The way he pulled back in his doorway, I
could tell he smelled death on my breath.
I'd always minted my mouth, always
ready to kiss my Prince when he arrived.
He never did. I'd worked on my muscles
dressed tight, went to the right discos, bars, clubs,
waiting. Instead I was kidnapped and robbed—
Then *this!* Because I was in medicine
I knew all the signs: no one else knew what I had—
the fevers, fatigue, breath like a sewer.
I sat a yard away from my lawyer as he handed
'round the will to first her, then him to sign.
They tried to make it light. Sweet of them.
But what did they know? . . . What I dread most is
when my relatives from Wyoming go through
my flat. Ask them to be careful. I have
eighteen thousand dollars worth of rare Ming
ware, collected in decades as I haunted
the aisles at Sotheby's, attended every
auction: it was all I ever loved.

# Minnie Bruce Pratt

## Night Gives Us the Next Day

*For Joan*

Tonight it is raining ice, no thunder, no light-
ning, just the cold rain hissing in the leaves.
Things are growing a skin of ice. Come close.
Warm my skin with the palm of your hand. I don't want
us brittle cold with pain. I want to dance
the flamingo with you, hot pink, and kiss.

The night weather is changeable as us: a kiss
of ice, then thunder, now melting rain, light
tongues whispering in the air: will we dance?
will we fight? You tell me of a lover who leaves
you: you won't leave me. But I've felt your want
change, shut tight against me, felt your heart close.

And me? Yes, I'm one afraid to be close.
I've said so. Have I said I'm afraid to lose one kiss
of yours? I've known how I'd love if I let myself want.
This is what I want: to be with you in slant light
shifting weather, morning, evening, forever: neither leaves
the other: so unlikely. But will you save a dance?

and we could do the duck, the raccoon, the fish: dance
thighs pressed against cunts: absolutely too close
for public. But not for the bar: The Other Side leaves
the lights down low: we could do more than kiss,
oh yes, we could practice who leads, how a light
hand, a supple back lead wherever they want:

to the car, to make out, make love, drive if we want,
midnight to the coast, hear the rain's uneven dance
in the marshes at dawn by Pamlico Sound: light
no fire, but watch in the grey, huddled close,

for flocks of islands, the wintering ducks: kiss
at the clap of their wings: thunder and night leaves:

leaves us together, not waked from a dream: leaves
us the next day, the days after. Say that's what you want.
There's still 15th Street, where we managed to kiss
in a grey drift of tear gas: we've yet to dance
there: or the streets where women pull blankets close,
sleep on islands of steam to live through to light.

Tonight rain in the street leaves cold hope that the woman will dance.
But we've worked more than change in the weather by stubborn want. Close
your arms around me, kiss me. We'll tell secrets on the world until light.


## Red String

At first she thought the lump in the road
was clay thrown up by a trucker's wheel:
then Beatrice saw the mess of feathers.
Six or seven geese stood in the right-of-way,
staring at the blood, their black heads
rigid above white throats. Unmoved
by passing wind or familiar violence,
they fixed their gaze on dead flesh
and something more, a bird on the wing.

It whirled into the thicket of fog that grew
up from fields plowed and turned to winter.
It joined other spirits exhaled just before dawn
from the rows of clay, creatures that had once
crept or flapped or crawled over the land,
twists of slime mold, coils of moccasin,
each gliding now in the life called death.

Beatrice had heard her mother tell of men
who passed as spirits. They hid in the limestone caves
by the river, hooded themselves inside the curved muscle,
the glistening wall of rock. Then just at dark
they appeared as if they had the power to slit the earth

open to release them. White robed, faceless horns for heads,
they advanced with torches over the water, saying
they were the ghosts of Shiloh and Bull Run fight.

Neighbors who watched at the bridge knew each man
by his voice or limp or mended boots but said
nothing, allowed the marchers to pass on: they ran
their skinny hounds to hunt other beings
into ravines, to keep flesh, darkness and death
another night distant from themselves, to save
their white skins from the carrion beetles,
spotted with red darker than blood, who wait
near the grave for the body to return to black earth.

Some Octobers the men killed scores, treed them
in the sweetgums, watched the face of a beast
flicker beside the starry purple-black leaves;
then they burned the tree. Smoke from their fires
still lay over the land where Beatrice travelled.
Out of this cloud the dead of the field spoke to her,
three voices from the place where women's voices never stop:

> They took my boy down by Sucarnochee creek.
> He said, "gentlemen, what have I done?"
> They says, "Never mind what you have done:
> we just want your damned heart." After they
> killed him, I built up a little fire and laid out
> by him all night until the neighbors came
> in the morning. I was standing there
> when they killed him, down by Sucarnochee creek.
> I am a mighty brave woman, but I was getting
> scared the way they were treating me, throwing rocks
> on my house, coming in disguise. They come to my bed
> where I was laying, and whipped me. They dragged me
> out into the field so that the blood strung across
> the house, and the fence, and the cotton patch,
> in the road, and they ravished me. Then they went
> back into my house and ate the food on the stove.

*They have drove me from my home. It is over*
*by DeSotoville, on the other side in Choctaw.*

*I had informed of persons whom I saw*
*dressing in Ku Klux disguise;*
*had named the parties. At the time*
*I was divorced from Dr. Randall*
*and had a school near Fredonia.*
*About one month before the election*
*some young men about the county*
*came in the night-time; they said*
*I was not a decent woman; also*
*I was teaching radical politics.*
*They whipped me with hickory withies*
*so the gashes cut through*
*my thin dress into the abdominal wall.*
*I was thrown into a ravine*
*in a helpless condition.*
*The school closed after my death.*

From the fog above the bloody entrails of the bird
the dead flew toward Beatrice like the night crow
whose one wing rest on the evening
while the other dusts off the morning star.
They gave her a jet-black look and said:

    *Child, what have you been up to while we*
    *were trying to keep body and soul together?*

    *But never mind that now. Here's what you must do:*

    *Tie a red flannel string around your waist*
    *for strength. Dig your roots*
    *at the dark of the moon. Remember your past,*
    *and ours. Always remember who you are.*
    *Don't let the men fool you about the ways of life*
    *even if blood must sign your name.*

# Eugene B. Redmond

## Epigrams for My Father

*(John Henry Redmond, Sr.)*

### I

*Fatherlore*: papa-rites, daddyhood;
   Run & trapsong: Search & dodgesong.
*Steelhammeringman.*
Gunbouter; whiskeywarrior.
*Nightgod!*
Moonballer/brawler grown old.
Slaughterhouse/river mackman:
Hightale teller & totempoleman.

### II

Wanderer across waters:
Folkbrilliance & Geniusgrit;
Railraging railsplitter:
Railrage! Railrage!
*IC & BM&O & MoPac & Midnight Special:*
Freight train . . . . . . bring my daddy back!

### III

Stone-story. The story of stone, brokenbricks—
Rocks hurled in pleasure & rage,
Pebbles soft & silent:
Home-dome is a blues-hard head.

IV

45-degree hat, Bulldurham butt bailing from lips;
Gabardine shining shining shining
Above white silk socks—
    satin man
    satin man
    silksure & steelstrong
    *hammerhold on life*
    *hammerhold on life*


V

Sun-son. Stonebone. Blackblitz.
*Fatherlore.* Struggledeep: Afridark, Afrolark,
    *daddydepth*—
    *Riverbottom song.*

# Louis Reyes Rivera

## I care about whichever word

I care about whichever word
is used like grass
or turned to twist
& make a victim look like killer
or heard to sing like daybreak
                        smelling . . .

An octorose of warmth
blending
into
nightshed
deep
a dance of waves
the sun weaves in
an intricate of light
            of gentle ripples
                warmly dancing
                weaving waves
            of shadelit haze
like the sea ebbing into shore.

Even in the repetition,
a word
means just as much to me
as morning's mist to dawn
the ease with which
            night
            moves
                    out
for daylight rays
like the quick shot from a gun

or loosely lipping attitude
that can just as easily
        grit
        or
        grin
        or
smile right back
in hard soft sounds
like a kitten's tender touch
a curious tiny paw wanting
but to be believed.


I like the word, determination,
a Black child learning how to read
the wonder of a family intact,
a puertorican
grasping & digging
into our own past . . . becoming Borinqueño
           studying Betances
                Belvis
                Pachin Marin
           listening to Malcolm
           hard
           intent
     & full of care
           concern
in a loving nudge of words
        penetrating
        deep inside the heart of thought
           with
        Yes! Of course!
           We got no choice
           but grow!
           & Be!
      & Stand Up, Child . . .
Come & Change this world
with strength & perseverance
Come & Grace this Earth

with your own sense longing
like the octorose of warmth

    u

      n

     f

      o

      l

       d

        i

      n

        g

winglike petals    unto dawn
           to soar, Yes, flying!


I like to hear Rashidah speak
I like to watch Zizwe's walk
    the happenstance of Sekou's song
    the lilting lyric in Safiya's sway
(& in case you do not know,
have never heard or watched them work:
Rashidah is an Ismaili,

           a misspelled word
           from the ink of census takers
           conquering her land;
           Zizwe, a child returned
           from whence once stole,
           Ngafua now an African at war;
           Sekou but a blue lake
           reclaiming lineage to Sundiata,
           undercoat guerilla born;
           Safiya, black pearl caught
           in the devil's hand
           way back when Hendersons
               cut loose from prison cells,
           sailed across atlantic gates
           to rape the earth into a world
           where poets have no chance).

Despite it all, they sing & work,
they write & read,
they care,
        get drunk
        or pray,
while few will publish them their due,
fewer still will plant their books
into your hands,
your own callouses of soil
                    digging
                    deep
                        into
                            self
gripping all their pages,
holding them as dearly as you would
an octorose of warmth.


& yes
I like the word of action true
the sound of gunfire busting through
                            the doors
that hold back freedom blue
        given
        how
our own young Blackfolk
get cornered into hating what to do
like Larry Davis
                cracking
                    through
                the wall of crack
                that would diffuse
whatever life a child could cling to /
cornered
in a vacuum of tenements jammed in despair
surrounded by a dozen cops
                a dozen watchful dogs
                    hunting
                            those who break
                    the must
                    & misty stink of deprivation


243

surrounded by a dozen cops
        alone
except for rifle
        shotgun
        millimeter
        automatic in his hand
bursting through the door
this five foot four
Davis,
Larry
     hurls across a rooftop
     shooting
     wounding
     striking out against
     this hateful passion
            cold
            city
            bred
escaping into freedom's scent

like the octorose of warmth
   s
    p
     r
      e
       a
        d
         i
          n
           g
             w    i    d    e
   its span of wings
   & soaring, Yes,
     soaring high & bleeding from the heart
                      of nothing
                      wanting
                      something
                      in the anywake
                      of every word
struggling for the worth of hope that comes at dawn.

# Al Robles

## Chinaman

Chinaman
remember!

Confucious was benevolent
and told you to behave

to be patient
to move along quietly
with great propriety

but one day
Lao Tzu came along

kicked his ass

and brought

the waterbuffalo ass
back to life

erected it high
up to the sun

pissed yellow seeds
of life

that spread
in an open valley
of free rebels

growing wild flowers
in the minds
of the people

children turned around
and caught the east wind
with their hands

opened their mouths wide
so the vegetables & rice
could drop in
just right
from the sky.


## Biographical Notes

Wendy Yoshimura
Nihonjin: Japanese
Sansei: 3rd Generation

Manzanar child
born 1943
Manzanar concentration camp
33 years ago

Japan bound
    etajima
small island
near hiroshima

       Wendy yoshimura
       windy  yoshiiiiiimuuuuuurra
                yoshiiiiiimuuuuuurra

         rise sad chrysanthemum
         behind the barbwire fence
         kiss the moon

            sharp bayonets cannot
              touch your face

windy yosshhiiimuuura
          yoshiimmmuuuuura

    heavy wind-bound cicada
    silk wings cannot be caught
    behind steel bars

    heavy wind-bound cicada
    steel bar cannot hold
    you down.


## Boyang the Wandering Recluse

Boyang-Boyang-Boyang-Boyang-Boyang
The northern wind sweeps the mind clear
into a thousand dreams, drawing Boyang
farther & farther & deeper & deeper into
the "snows of life." His bamboo flute
cuts across the thick icebergs—vibra-
ting layers of the mind that circle the
Bering Sea. Loneliness grabs the heart,
filling it with burning portraits of "wo-
men of the past." How many women have
given up their lives for you? Their minds
sweetened your taste buds—their pale bodies
clung to your wandering bamboo flute.

    Boyang-Boyang-Boyang-Boyang-Boyang
    How deep is the silence in winter?
    How far is the journey?
    When the paths covered in snow
    No longer welcome the ancient songs
    Your long bamboo flute brings back snow-memories
    Has the snow fallen anew?
    Mountains grow tall and sad
    Flowers waiting to bloom

Frozen-silence
Still-dreams
Boyang-Boyang-Boyang-Boyang-Boyang
The snow's still thick around
Your bamboo flute.

# Aleida Rodríguez

## The Island of the Living

First we hear the bone-on-bone of skeletons dancing
followed by the droning voices of an all-male choir
like the soundtrack of a fifties horror movie
when fear, like everything else, was less complicated.
That's why the monsters are no longer convincing to us:
zippers showing, they are someone's friends dressed
for Halloween.

But the music sings discordantly to another part of us
of the unresolved things we churn into daily nightmares:
the myths about ourselves that slowly decompose
into banal horror films with us as shallow actors
reenacting our deepest fears in grainy black and white.

Every once in a while there's a sound like a drum
stretched from the skin of our bellies. But then
the skeletons come dancing back in, playing piccolos
and accompanying themselves with their own clack-clacks.
If it weren't so mediocre, it would terrify us.

## Epiphany

*For Caesar*

*I'm worried about Bill Manzana,* he said. He was spinning around his white
kitchen on one of the hottest days of the year. Shutting drawers, sliding knives
into their wooden rack.

*What now.* I was leaning against the wall trying to cool myself, looking out
the kitchen window at the driveway filled with old cars.

*He's shooting.*

*Great.* I said, not turning around. I wanted to know what kind of cars they were. One was fifties; it glinted its silver teeth at me. And they were all covered with peaches, peaches that had fallen from the tree overhanging the driveway.

The cars cradled them on their heads and laps as though still offering them to someone. Forget it in this heat. The sun was burning a tiny yellow laser through each one of them.

*Wow. Look at all those rotting peaches,* I said.

*Yeah,* he said. *Isn't that incredible.*

# Kate Rushin

## Why I Like to Go Places: Flagstaff, Arizona—June 1978

*To wander is to lodge. To lodge is to become familiar with
strange places.*

I Ching

I was not supposed to go places
I was not supposed to go off the block
To The Park
To Bad Parts of town
Or to places I'd never been before
I was not supposed to hitchhike
Or go into bars like Langston Hughes did
And talk to men like Simple
Why can't I go? Why can't I go?
(Of course I knew why. Everybody knows why.)

But still I had to go
And that is why I bought a
$69 Anywhere-We-Go bus ticket
And that is how I came to meet George Pryor
Formerly of Mobile, Alabama
Proprietor of the Rio Grand Motel
Coach of the Front End Alignments
Women's softball team and his daughter Janie
And his son-in-law Danny and his other kids
And his little grand' Puddin
This is how George came to tell me in a
Slightly perplexed voice
How his 19-year-old daughter and her husband
Were poisoned by a gas leak in a borrowed apartment
On Christmas and weren't found until 2 days later
This is how I came to fix fried chicken and biscuits for George
A 42-year-old Black construction worker in Flagstaff, Arizona
With a family of 6 there and a family of 7 in Mobile
I also fixed dinner for Ira

The wizened alcoholic white man who lives with him and
Watches the place during the day and worships the ground
He walks on

This is how I came to read the letter that Ira's
Diabetic adopted granddaughter had written him from the reformatory
And how I told Ira
Sure she'll come back
As the tears rolled down the furrows of his cheeks

And this is how I came to sit in the car at the game
With George and his friend Bobby drinking beer
While Bobby told how Ellie's boy
The one who had got put out on the street
Was found dead in an abandoned house and nobody knew why
Except it mighta been drugs or pneumonia or a combination of both
And George shook his head and sighed and figured it didn't do any good
To talk about it

This is how I came to be riding around in the car with George
And up to the top of the hill over-looking the city
And past the University where his wife works as a secretary
And this is how I came to be sitting in the Homeward Bound Bar
Listening to George talk about his wife and his kids and his girlfriend
And his buddy Gerald who got shot in the back of the head by
A white policeman who said Gerald was coming at him with a gun
And how that policeman knows that George knows
Who murdered his buddy
And how George himself did time
And he didn't want to do it
But the boy wouldn't back off
And that's how he ended up leaving Mobile

And this is how George came to say
Shall I call you in the morning
Or shall I lean over and just whisper
I said
Call me George

And then in the morning George said
I think I'm sick

I don't think I need to go to work today
Don't I look sick to you
I said George
You look fine
And then we had breakfast and then I was off to the Canyon
And then to L.A.

And all that is why I carry a picture of a gold-toothed
Black man from Flagstaff, Arizona wearing a suit and tie
And stingy-brim hat

That is why I carry a picture of George in my wallet.


## The Black Back-Ups

This is dedicated to Merry Clayton, Cissy Houston, Vonetta Washington, Dawn, Carrietta McClellen, Rosie Farmer, Marsha Jenkins and Carolyn Williams. This is for all of the Black women who sang back-up for Elvis Presley, John Denver, James Taylor, Lou Reed, Etc. Etc. Etc.

I said Hey Babe
Take a walk on the Wild Side
I said Hey Babe
Take a walk on the Wild Side

And the colored girls say

Do dodo do do dodododo
Do dodo do do dodododo
Do dodo do do dodododo ooooo

This is for my greatgrandmother Esther, my grandmother Addie, my grandmother called Sister, my great Aunt Rachel, my aunt Hilda, my aunt Tine, my aunt Breda, my cousin Barbara, my cousin Dottie and my great great aunt Rebe

This is dedicated to all of the Black women riding on buses and subways back and forth to the Main Line, Haddonfield, N.J. Cherry Hill and Chevy Chase. This is for those women who spend their summers in Rockport, Newport,

Cape Cod, and Camden, Maine. This is for those women who open those
bundles of dirty laundry sent home from those Ivy-covered campuses

And the colored girls say

Do dodo do do dodododo
Do dodo do do dodododo
Do dodo do do dodododo ooooo

Jane Fox     Jane Fox
Calling Jane Fox
Where are you Jane?

My Great Aunt Rachel worked for the Foxes
Ever since I can remember
There was The Boy
Whose name I never knew
And there was The Girl
Whose name was Jane

My Aunt Rachel brought Jane's dresses for me to wear
Perfectly Good Clothes
And I should've been glad to get them
Perfectly Good Clothes
No matter they didn't fit right
Perfectly Good Clothes Jane
Brought home in a brown paper bag with an air of
Accomplishment and excitement
Perfectly Good Clothes
Which I hated

It's not that I have anything *personal* against *you* Jane
It's just that I felt guilty
For hating those clothes
I mean can you get to the irony of it Jane?

And the colored girls say

Do dodo do do dodododo
Do dodo do do dodododo
Do dodo do do dodododo ooooo

At school in Ohio
I swear to Gawd
There was always somebody
Telling me that the only person
In their whole house
Who listened to them and talked to them
Despite all of the money and the lessons
Was the housekeeper
And I knew it was true
But what was I supposed to say?

I know it's true
I watch them getting off the train
And moving slowly toward the Country Squire
With their uniform in their shopping bag
And the closer they get to the car
The more the two little kids jump and laugh
And even the dog is about to
Turn inside out
Because they just can't wait until she gets there
Edna Edna     Wonderful Edna
(But Aunt Edna to me, or Gram, or Miz Johnson, or Sister Johnson on
    Sundays)

And the colored girls say

Do dodo do do dodododo
Do dodo do do dodododo
Do dodo do do dodododo ooooo

This is for Hattie McDaniels, Butterfly McQueen, Ethel Waters
Saphire
Saphronia
Ruby Begonia
Aunt Jemima
Aunt Jemima on the Pancake Box
Aunt Jemima on the Pancake Box?
AuntJemimaonthepancakebox?
auntjemimaonthepancakebox?
Ainchamamaonthepancakebox?
Ain't chure Mama on the pancake box?

Mama Mama
Get offa that damn box
And come home to me
And my Mama leaps offa that box
She swoops down in her nurse's cape
Which she wears on Sunday
And on Wednesday night prayer meeting
And she wipes my forehead
And she fans my face for me
And she makes me a cup o' tea
And it don't do a thing for my real pain
Except she is my Mama
Mama mommy mommy mammy mammy
Mam-my mam-my
I'd Walk a mill-yon miles
For one o' your smiles

This is for the Black Back-Ups
This is for my mama and your mama
My grandma and your grandma
This is for the thousand thousand Black Back-Ups

And the colored girls say

Do dodo     do  do     dodododo
Do         do  do     do    do
   Do              do                 do


Do                          do

## Words

We had more than
we could use.
They embarrassed us,
our talk fuller than our
rooms. They named
nothing we could see—
*dining room, study,*
*mantel piece, lobster*
*thermidor.* They named
things you only
saw in movies—
the thin flicker Friday
nights that made us
feel empty in the cold
as we walked home
through our only great
abundance, snow.
This is why we said "ain't"
a "he don't."
We wanted words to fit
our cold linoleum,
our oil lamps, our
outhouse. We knew
better but it was wrong
to use a language
that named ghosts,
nothing you could touch.
We left such words at school
locked in books
where they belonged.
It was the vocabulary
of our lives that was
so thin. We knew this
and grew to hate

all the words that named
the vacancy of our rooms—
looking here we said
*studio couch* and saw cot;
looking there we said
*venetian blinds* and saw only the yard;
*brick* meant tarpaper,
*fireplace* meant wood stove.
And this is why we came to love
the double negative.


## Washrags

In Long Valley the Finns
Brought the old country with them
Brought it in the 'nineties
In steerage in their ragged luggage
They lugged it with them
It was a millstone and the knives in their boots
It was the way they stood around
The store in town
Eyes down shoulders hunched
Waiting for everyone else to buy
They packed it with them in gunny sacks
They took it to dances
Condensed and distilled
In pint bottles
They beat each other with it
Behind Finn Hall
Its weight pulled
Them out of school at fourteen
It ruined their teeth with hardtack
And filled their mouths
With strange accents
No soap would wash loose
It was the broken axle and the bad crop
It was the huge tree
They knew would fall
They smiled grimly

Knowing 1929 by its real name
It let the traveling dentist
Pull all my grandfather's teeth
The year he died
It was in the washrag I buried
For my father
To cure a wart

# Primus St. John

## Reading a Story to My Child

This is a small boy
In a ragged coat.
Moving through his world
Is a bold paint brush
Briefing on the light in the dark.

In the most subtle way
You are drawn to the heart
Because the heart is the name
Of the story
But you do not know this yet.

He is going to school:
Though you know he must first
Cross the lake,
Whistle to the birds,
And clean out an understanding path
In the tall grass.

He is a good boy
Who adores crows;
He even talks like them.

He is no fool;
He will not hurt you.
He does not talk;
He lives an honest life.

At school, the children
Abhor him.
They see clothes
And the disaster of no voice.

What kind of school is this
That abhors true love?

He may not eat much,
But they are starved.
*Boy*, you are in the tall grass
And the soil is ruthless.

What do they teach here
That is as nice as our eyes closed?
The school is on a strange page
Farther away than the lines of the smallest trees.
And each parted brush stroke
Is like a squadron of geese.

But the little boy holds on
To his heart.
(*Yes Sir*) It is better than a bright nickel,
Or a ball,
Or a tall pole.

He does not know
Quite how to write.
He thinks language
Is a series of bizarre pictures.

Though it is loud
It is not sharp like a crow's voice CAW CAW CAW.
And it is not bright
Like a birthday of new flowers.
(*Yes Sir*)
In all of the fields that he knows,
These pictures are not wise—
And he knows this.

At a certain point, there is more
Color on the page

Than in the eyes of a dove
Who is listening.

He looks out of the window—
Home.
Someone there who knows him—
Softly and hard
Sees our storm,
Its ruthlessness
And its subtle tentacle of rain
We have all absorbed.

Hey,
But this is a boy who holds on.
My, you'd want to know this boy.
Now I am on page 8
And afraid for my soul.
At this point I say,
Boy,
(*Yes Sir*)
I say, Boy
Hold on for us all.

But today, he is given a brush.
He has climbed all the way down
And he has climbed back up
On this strange way that gets here,
And because he is not afraid
Darkness does not hide him.
He knows its crows
And there love is prehistoric

Like shale at the gorge,
Like evening cold,
Like the lonely gills of a fat fish
At the edge of water.

My, My, My,
You'd love this boy
Just for how it feels.

He paints birds at that
Exact moment flight enflames us.
He sees their heads as small prayers
On the lips of the sky.

(*Yes Sir*)
He knows how—this boy;
He knows how their wings are
Soft, ironic smiles that are alive.

My, My, My,
How daddy cries (*Yes Sir*).
This here is just a boy he knows
And won't say why.
A small boy
In a rugged coat.


## Biological Light

We live here to eat;
Things stare at us.
Those things eat.
We call all of this hunger
The world.
Why?
Because we live here . . .

All over the world
Morning light is still happening
Like God.
It is so hard to tell
Who eats the plants first—
        Insects or crepuscular.

The wind feels the smallest birds
It's not a lot—
Here comes the fox.

Noon: circles logically like the hawk.
God moves the rim around
Until the fox is in.
Now the fox is the hawk
And all the small things he ate
Believe him . . .

I have come here late;
The deer look like they have gone,
But thorns remind me
More is going on.

Gradually, memory sets the table back,
I have come from,
Across the water, as far back,
As I can know.
Friends there have eaten me;
Now I stand here, that torn by hate
As I myself have eaten them.

Late; the owls say whooo
For what more will surely come.
Finally, I am older—
But not enough—
Surrounded by what I know
Is falling back toward the grass
More like luck than hope . . .

I am just lying here
Thinking this in my sleep—
How cold it is outside.
If we were fish where it is very dark
It would all be so easy
Light would come from the dead things that we eat.

# Cheryl Savageau

## Henri Toussaints

When Henri Toussaints
came down from Quebec
his hands already knew
the fine shape of the world
the hungry feel of earth
eager to be sown
the wet hard flank of a mare
the proper curve of a cradleboard.

His hands had eased the young
from sheep and mares
had freed the bound egg
and women
with no doctor about
with the pains coming close
wanted his hands
to navigate the maze
to bring the child
to first light.

Later the husbands would say
come, Henri, to dinner
eat with us, Henri
and they would sit to table
for the coming of new life
demands great things.

Later, much later,
Rosa had
cried out on the marriage bed
and the blood had come
red and strong and not stopping
as if getting were as hard as birthing.

He had soothed her then as if
she were one of his fine
mares, had crooned
Rosa, ma pauvre, Rosa, ma poule,
til she had quieted
and the bleeding stopped.

She brought him his first son
head so small it barely filled his palm
too small to live, they told him
but in the box behind the stove
next to the steaming kettle
and with Rosa's good milk
the boy had thrived.

Still when Henri held him
he sang Il p'tit, Rosa, he's small,
and so they called him,
though his name was Armand
and he grew to be a man large
of hand and chest
still they called him Ipsy
from his father.

And others followed:
Marie, called Tootsie, all small,
Eva, 'tipoule, little chicken,
and Peter who was called Bébé,
though more were born after him,
eight in all, and Baby Alice,
who was born with red curls
and a hole in her heart.

Cold spring nights
the hole grew grave-size
settled in his own heart
mocked his healer's hands.

In the kitchen at night
with the oil lamp burning

he placed the fine gears
into the ancient watch.

The priests are wrong, Rosa,
it is not in the heart
that the soul lives,
but here,
in the hands.


## Bones—A City Poem

forget the great blue heron flying low
    over the marsh, its footprints
    still fresh in the sand

forget the taste of wild mushrooms
    and where to find them

forget lichen-covered pines
    and iceland moss

forget shaking wild rice into your canoe

forget the one-legged duck
    and the eggs of the snapping turtle
    laid in the bank

forget the frog found in the belly of a bass

forget the cove testing its breath
    against the autumn morning

forget the down-filled nest
    and the snake swimming at midday

forget the bullhead lilies
    and the whiskers
    of the pout

forget walking on black ice
    beneath the sky hunter's bow

forget the living waters
    of Quinsigamond

forget how to find the Pole star and why

forget the eyes of the red fox
    the hornets that made their home
    in the skull of a cow

forget waking to hear the call of the loon

forget that raccoons are younger brothers
    to the bear

forget that you are walking
    on the bones of your grandmothers

# Ron Schreiber

## four ways of silence

### 1

when starlings cluster
under the bridges, one

flock of noise, to hover
above a barge in the down-

stream channel, a crow
over the Hudson.

### 2

I screamed at you last night,
repeatedly, & you

didn't say anything

### 3

when we make love, I never
whisper in your ear, never

speak to you or utter word
sounds, you murmur sometimes

or that's the way I remember
when we used to make love

together, but we don't talk
about that now.

4

coming towards each other
on the open beach, the sun

shining, the sea calm for a change.
between us is a spot of silence

we enter together
simultaneously.


## what you're teaching me

I already knew the principles of a perennial garden:
tall flowers at the back, smallest in the front;
season-long bloom from hyacinths & crocus
to great bushy mums; and the right colors.

what I didn't know except for spring (I'd
lived in Holland) was all the particulars:
the quince, the varieties of iris,
delicate Japanese peonies,
giant auratum lilies & tetraploid daylilies,
purple-to-blue delphinium in my own garden.

or how to care & not to care, how to experiment
—if something dies in sandy soil or
if the rabbits eat it, how to try something
else in the same place; or how to move a plant
so it will get more sun.

how to be patient:
if dogwood seedlings bloom ten years from now
they will have pink blossoms.

planting—you seem to know—is letting things
happen in their own time

or helping them when they need help
& listening attentively to what they say
even if they don't use words.


## they kill us

*For B. S.*

all the time. & some punk
tells the judge, "your honor,
that man was queer, he tried to . . ."

*what would you do if somebody tried to?*

if we're married they rape the wife
for good measure. there's pleasure
in kicking us when we're already

down. & if we're brown, some Secretary
of Agriculture will say, "you know,
there's only 3 things blacks want . . ."

*what would you do? if somebody*

befriended you but turned out to be
all 3? married & queer & black.
fuck the wife. stab the nigger in the back.

if it makes the papers, the papers will say,
"another random act of violence
came our way. yesterday."

*what would you do?*

## January, 1978

every day is Sunday now.
Monday it snowed, &
Tuesday everything stopped.
the trains stopped, the buses stopped, the
factories stopped, the hospitals almost
stopped & every day for a whole week
there was no traffic & people walked in the streets.

today is Saturday & the traffic is stopped.
tomorrow will really be Sunday.
the next day will be Monday &
it will snow again, &
just like last week it will snow again
all day Tuesday & everything will stop.
only this time there will be no place to put the snow.

this is the second winter of the apocalypse.
last winter was very cold.
this winter there is more snow than ever.
Tom's mother said there is all this snow in Boston
because Tom is queer, but last winter
the orange crop froze in Florida.
& it snowed in Albany where Tom's mother called from
& will snow again Monday & Tuesday

& break record after record.
some people will say it snows because we are queer.
others will say it snows because the northeast
is a decadent part of the country.
but it is really snowing because
this is the second winter of the apocalypse,

which is coming in ice & cold.
this winter there are mudslides in California.
last winter there was drought.
& next winter the earth will open over the
San Andreas fault like it has opened in Turkey
& Guatemala City. the apocalypse

is not one gigantic tragedy,
it comes a winter at a time,

then a summer at a time, & people don't say,
—oh, the world is ending. they blame the snowfalls
on the queers, who are suddenly everywhere,
dancing on the rim of the earth,
making love while the sun still shines.

# Susan Sherman

## Definitions

### 1

I think it's coming close to death
that does it
           both others
   & your own
that magnifies the values
begins the definitions

This morning
           mild at last
   after weeks of chill
Streets heavy with water
People stepping
           cautiously
   hardly knowing where
   to place their feet
so accustomed to barriers
             of salt and ice

My mind resembles those winter streets
grey
   with sludge
The snow cover melted
The sidewalks washed of unfamiliar
glare

### 2

After all     she said
What difference does it make?

That's the reason I never write
hardly speak     of what is me

I begin to answer glibly     stop
Held myself in identical fear
My own touch tentative
                    almost an excuse
like making love to someone
for the first time
or the third     (which is always harder)
once you begin to know     experience
another
        the tension of your hair     brown
        streaked with grey
                        the lines of
        your face     like wires     rushing through
        your forehead     your knees


        3

Warm outside     the steam
continues     forced by habit
I open the window     throw the
oracle     trace the heat
*The heart thinks constantly* it says
One constant then     the heart     another
the drawing back
                Four o'clock
two hours till dawn     Nightmare
image     your face
surrounded by strangers
Beloved     you turn
                    away


Sweat mixes with flowered sheets
The constant fear
                To push out
finally     cautiously     tentatively
and find
        an empty place

Death brings us close to it
Death itself
        forgetting
And we the living
wanting to remember
not wishing to be forgotten
                   separated
from what we hold most near

I hold you for a moment     lose you
watch you disappear
               I hold you
for a lifetime     lose you

the next year     the next morning
the next minute     the next breath

5

You tell me
What can I say to that
young woman 18 years
of age?

That I at 38 must once more lay aside
all sense of definition     order
Must once more carefully measure
the accumulation of my years

Or should I say
her question can be answered
in specific needs     others
and her own
             But she's asking
more than that     We both know
what she means

The only real difference being death
The one who stops the heart

# Beverlyjean Smith

## Cool

Measure his strides by the length of the arm's arc:
an oar pushing his     spirit through space. His knee
dipping like a ripple ripples

nudging his     right shoulder back, cushioning
his shoe into a step: heel ball as the left foot
taps through on the count of three

just when the sidewalk's hard silence
needs touching. For a split second his arm and hand
sag like the curve of cold molasses then strokes the air

again. He glides, head tilted just so the     eyes
look asleep. His ear rests on the edge of the city.
Inside the horn's blare, he hears muted chords.

Brakes screech, wild birds caress     leaves darken
as shadows hunch. a prowling cat. He smiles
falls into an art form black men have learned to perfect.


## Wash Days

Grandma Harriet
pushes her white tub machine
on summer days
when the sun can fry eggs
and all the grandchildren chew ice.

She assembles the tools of her trade:
wicker baskets, a wooden framed scrub board and three tubs
for rinsing, bluing and starching.
In two large pots

she runs tap water from the one silver spout
extended over the deep tin sink
then sets them on the black top stove.

The vapor takes away her breath.
Veiled in steam,
the ritual begins:
Dish towel bandages protect her baking hands
as she hobbles shooing us behind her.
Hot water swooshes into the tub
pulls beads of tears out of grandma's skin.

Waiting
for the old rollers to nibble the ends of garments
Grandma will feed it
I think of the white ladies who drop off their loads
and the lips of the machine
when it ate Cousin Goochie's
fingers, hand and arm lifeless
as their twisting sleeves
before the washer choked
on his pain.

# Carmen Tafolla

## How Shall I Tell You?

*listening to the news, the U.S. attack on Libya, the Soviet nuclear accident at Chernobyl . . .*

When no soul walks the softened green
and no foot beats the pulse on crumbling brown
and no one lives to sing to rain
or soak to sun the spirit of its golden gown
to weave the many colors of the after-arch
from sky to human skin to wooded wealth
in fiber fabrics beads and tusks and seeds
all leading up in rows of beauty drumbeat
to black neck, like venison in stealth

When no one lulls the child to sleep
or takes the wrinkled story's hand
or listens to the news—a wired sound
of tribe on tribe—stet now—man on man
How shall I tell you that I love you then?
How shall I touch your fingers tip to tip
   and say that we were blood and human voice and friend?

## October 21st, 9 P.M. (autumn she don't waste no time!)

*(to the autumn night sky)*

. . . and the night gets sassy again
      and says "no way" she's gonna act hot and white
                        (or even hi yeller)
      when she's *really* feelin cool and dark and slinky.

No way she's gonna dress up soft, light, sophisticated
                                        and polite
    when she's really sharply naked, lustily growin'
    at the middle, and with every single freckle
    of a star
    showin clear through
                        (—and no makeup to boot!)

. . . she gets sassy,
        starts breathin' October-like—


                    shivery and ripe,


                late harvest of a lady,
                no springtime gentle flower
                but one whose womb has swollen
                and whose heart has broken
                and whose spirit has picked up
                and moved on, and grown fuller,
                                    older,
                                    proud.


. . . the night, she gets sassy,
    ready to move up, or move on,
    but *move!*—no standin still
        she don't keep life
        she swallows it
        gustily


            drops wiped off with a sleeve
            don't wait for table napkins
                    —they come too late—
            Drink life 'n' laugh
            'n' let it go unreined
            let it be what it will be
                            she says

. . . and her breezes pant strong
  she works hard
    plays hard
     breathes deep

      blows the useless stuff away—
           like leaves
            from seasons
     looks to the root       past
     goes for the gut

     lays her earthy soul

     right up against her lover-man earth

       with nothin'

        in

       between'm.

## The Boy

Looking back,
I think that he must have been an angel.
We never spoke,
but one entire summer, every day,
he sat on the curb across the street.
I watched him: thin, his skin white,
his blond hair cut short.
Sometimes, right after swimming,
his bathing suit wet and tight,
he would sit and dry off in the sun.
I couldn't stop staring.

Then late one night,
toward the end of the summer,
he appeared in my room.
Perhaps that's why
I've always considered him
an angel: silent, innocent, pale
even in the dark.
He undressed
and pulled back the sheet,
slid next to me.
His fingers felt for my lips.

But perhaps I am not remembering
correctly.
Perhaps he never came
into my room that night.
Perhaps he never existed
and I invented him.
Or perhaps it was me, not blond
but dark, who sat all summer
on that sunny corner: seventeen
and struggling to outlast
my own restlessness.

## Impressions 15

bright day in pennsylvania
steel blue
                    the mountains clear
from here & out hear cold
the naked sky
soft at duskglow when the sun
sinks clear down

through winter trees bare
skin leaves shake down

                    snow mounds cover
the ground & footprints
like inked words on white pages
print themselves
into snow

stretch themselves around
& into dark, awesome
silence, grows
into this
terrible world


## Poem for My Father; For Quincy Trouppe, Sr.

father, it was an honor to be there, in the dugout
with you, the glory of great black men swinging their lives
as bats at tiny white balls
burning in at unbelievable speeds, riding up & in & out
a curve falling off the table, moving away screwing its stitched
magic into chitlin circuit air, its comma seams spinning
towards break down, dipping, like a hipster

bebopping a knee-dip stride in the charlie parker forties
wrist curling behind a "slick" black back
like a swan's neck, cupping
an invisible ball of dreams—

father, & you there regal as an african obeah man sculpted
out of wood, from a tree of no name no place origin
thick roots branching down into cherokee & someplace else lost
way back in africa, the sap running dry
crossing from north carolina, into georgia, in grandmother mary's womb
your mother in the violence of that red soil, ink blotter
gone now into blood graves of american news sponging
rococo truth dead & long gone as dinosaurs
the agent-oranged landscape of former names
absent of polysyllables, dry husk consonants there
now, in their place, flat as polluted rivers
& that guitar string smile always snaking across virulent
american red neck faces scorching, like atomic
heat mushrooming over nagasaki & hiroshima
those fever blistered shadows of it all
inked into sizzling concrete

but you there father, a yardbird solo riffin on
bat & ball glory, breaking down the fabricated myths
of white major league legends, of who was better
than who, beating them at their own crap
game with killer bats, as bud powell swung his silence into beauty
of a josh gibson home run skittering across the piano keys
of bleachers, shattering all fabricated legends up there in lights
struck-out white knights running the risky edge of amazement
awe, the miraculous truth sluicing through
steeped in the blues, confluencing, like the point
at the cross between a fastball disguised as a curve
sliding away in a wicked sly grin, posed as an ass scratching
uncle tom, like satchel paige delivering his hesitation pitch,
then coming back with a hard high fast one
quicker than a professional hit-
man, the deadliness of it all, the strike

like that of the brown bomber's, or sugar
ray robinson's lightning, cobra bite

& you there father, catching rhythms of chano pozo
balls, drumming into your catcher's mitt
fast as "cool papa" bell jumping into bed
before the lights went out

of the old negro baseball league, a promise
a harbinger, of shock waves, soon to come

# Kitty Tsui

## Don't Let Them Chip Away at Our Language

haa-low, okay,
dank que, gut bye.

the only words
my grandmother knew.
the only words of english
she spoke
on a regular basis
in her rhythm of
city cantonese
mixed with
chinatown slang:
du pont guy,
low-see beef,
and, you good gel,
sic gee mah go,
sic apple pie
yum coca co-la.

a few proper nouns
were also part of
her vocabulary.
ny name, kit-ee
san fan-see,
pete gid-ding
her favorite
weatherman on tv,
say-fu-way
where she would
stock up on
rolls of toilet paper,

sponges and ajax.
on sale, of course.

in the spring of 1985
a republican assemblyman
proposed a bill
to make english
the official language
of the state.
his rationale:
we're no longer
going to let them
chip away at our language.
if they can't
understand english
they shouldn't be here
at all.

we first came
in 1785, three seamen
stranded in baltimore.
later we were
merchants and traders,
cooks and tailors,
contract laborers hired
to work in the mines,
in construction,
in the canneries,
hired to do what no man would:
hang from cliffs in a basket,
endure harsh winters
and blast through rock
to build the iron horse.

we became sharecroppers
growing peanuts,
strawberries,
cabbage and
chrysanthemums.
opened restaurants

and laundries,
worked in rich homes,
on ranches and farms
tending stock,
cleaning house,
cooking and ironing,
chopping firewood,
composing letters home
dreaming of a wife, a son.

we are tong yan,
american born
and immigrants
living in l.a., arizona,
brooklyn and the bronx,
san mateo and the sunset.
we eat burgers and baw,
custard tart and bubblegum.
we are doctors, actors,
artists, carpenters,
maids and teachers,
gay and straight.
we speak in many tongues:
sam yup, say yup, street talk,
the queen's english.

please don't let them
chip away at our language.

# Alma Villanueva

## The Harvest

1

They had forgotten
me when I
left and when I
returned seeking
the new connection,
the unfinished chain,
the city was always
as it was: cold
cement and the blossoms
bursting forth
in the prescribed
park, people
walking in circles
going somewhere
and they didn't
know or care
that I'd returned
with a new song
in my mouth, but
my eyes are open
now,
and the grey cement
melted in my fire:
where the cracks
are showing, small
flowers sing
through, and this
time
I am here to
hear everything
and what I see, I'll

note down, and then
when everything
is quite still
in that crack
I'll sing.


## 2

Who was that boy
I left?
Who was that girl
I left?
Is the shade still
up?
Is the water running?
Is the door locked?
Is the cat put
out?
Is the cement still
sleeping like a
long grey
feline, purring,
waiting
for the earthquake
to stroke its
belly? Wild
children still roam
the streets, shooting
rainbows from
their eyes.


## 3

The young have
a language that
excludes the
old. The old have
a language that
excludes all

life, and here
I am with
a mouthful
of fire.


                4


A man in jail
must imagine the
Earth or go
crazy. A woman
in her ninth
month, her child,
and I,
my voice: I
imagine you listening
there among the
stones, gathering
rainbows.


## The Flagrant Mala Puta*

The sound of Mexican music in
the middle of the day
brings me through
the door—my ancestors

leap out of my face
and hair, my body—
Yaqui, Spanish, German—
a graceful mix, I do not

bend, hide, but want
to sit among you—

*Flagrare, to burn—
more at BLACK: archaic,
FLAMING, GLOWING. . . .
Mala Puta, Bad Whore. . . .

women with their arms
and back tattooed entirely—

me with my small
rose perched on my
shoulder—women with
their middles coming

out of their midriffs,
me with my yoga
waist of champagne
and children,

and, yes, also
enchiladas, chorizo, Dos
Equis—a Mexican man,
unaware he is shorter

than me, asks me to
dance, and I do not
bend or hide, everyone
watching—he begins

to clutch my waist
and I gently put
his hand back in
mine—insulted, he

leaves me standing
tall, flagrant, free—
all the men knowing
he could not own me in

a million years—
a young black man
from Arkansas asks me
to dance, and I do—

    "I want ta be
    able ta come

and go, ya
know—I ain't

gonna live in
no swamps—
and I don't
give a damn

bout people's
color, we all
in it together—
d'ya know what

what I mean?"
"It's called
freedom."
He smiles broadly,

"Yeah," and we
dance again—
that night at my
reading some young

Mexican women ask
me to read a favorite
poem, and later
one of them tells

me her friends
call her Mala Puta
and the she intends
to name her first

book of poetry
Mala Puta—yes,
Màla Puta, never,
I repeat,

never,
belong to
anyone but
the fire.

293

# Tino Villanueva

## Scene from the Movie *Giant*

What I have from 1956 in one instant at the Holiday
Theater, where a small dimension of a film, as in
A dream, became the feature of the whole. It
Comes toward the end . . . the café scene, which
Reels off a slow spread of light, a stark desire

To see itself once more, though there is, at times,
No joy in old time movies. It begins with the
Jingling of bells and the plainer truth of it:
That the front door to a roadside café opens and
Shuts as the Benedicts (Rock Hudson and Elizabeth

Taylor), their daughter Luz, and daughter-in-law
Juana and grandson Jordy, pass through it not
Unobserved. Nothing sweeps us into an actual act
Of kindness into the eyes of Sarge, who owns this
Joint and has it out for dark-eyed Juana, weary

Of too much longing that comes with rejection.
Juana, from barely inside the door, and Sarge,
Stout and unpleased from behind his counter, clash
Eye-to-eye, as time stands like heat. Silence is
Everywhere, acquiring the name of hatred and Juana

Cannot bear the dread—the dark-jowl gaze of Sarge
Against her skin. Suddenly: bells go off again.
By the quiet effort of walking, three Mexican-
Types step in, whom Sarge refuses to serve . . .
Those gestures of his, those looks that could kill

A heart you carry in memory for years. A scene from
The past has caught me in the act of living: even
To myself I cannot say except with worried phrases

294

Upon a paper, how I withstood arrogance in a gruff
Voice coming with the deep-dyed colors of the screen;

How in the beginning I experienced almost nothing to
Say and now wonder if I can ever live enough to tell
The aftertale. I remember this and I remember myself
Locked into a backrow seat—I am a thin, flickering,
Helpless light, local-looking, unthought of at fourteen.


## The 8:00 O'Clock Movie

*Boston, 1973*—Years had passed and I assumed a
Different life when one night, while resting from
Books on Marlborough Street (where things like
This can happen), there came into my room images

In black-and-white with a flow of light that
Would not die. It all came back to me in different
Terms: characters were born again, met up with
Each other in adult life, drifted across the

Screen to discover cattle and oil, travelled miles
On horseback in dust and heat, characters whose
Names emerged as if they mattered in a history
Book. Some were swept up by power and prejudice

Toward neighbors different from themselves,
Because that is what the picture is about, with
Class distinctions moving the plot along. A few
Could distinguish right from wrong; those who

Could not you condemned from the beginning when
You noticed them at all. Still others married or
Backed off from the ranch with poignant flair,
Like James Dean, who in the middle of grazing land

Unearthed the treasures of oil, buried his soul in
Money and went incoherent with alcohol. When the 40s

Came, two young men were drafted, the one called *Angel*
Dying at war. It's a generational tale, so everybody

Aged once more and said what they had to say along the
Way according to the script. And then the end: the
Hamburger joint brought into existence to the beat of
"The Yellow Rose of Texas," Juana and her child the

Color of dark amber, foreshadowing the Mexican-looking
Couple and their daughter, all in muteness, wanting
To be served. I climbed out of bed and in my head
Was a roaring of light—words spoken and unspoken

Had brought the obliterated back. Not again (I said,
From my second-floor room) . . . let this not be happening.
Three-and-a-half hours had flicked by. As the sound
Trailed off into nothing, memory would not dissolve.

# Roberta Hill Whiteman

## No Longer

I no longer fear the firestorm despair.
Green earth has coaxed my soul
over a blue bridge of forget-me-nots,
into her hollow of oak leaves, lilies.
Now each creek I cross balances
dark and day as birds give no thought
to each wing's weight, but fly, singing.

I no longer expect the firestorm despair
to sear the ground I grow on.
Horns of sumac have broken my blindness.
Thunder's taste glitters on my lips.
The moon urges my blood root's burgeoning.
Her fierce song cools this light I feed on.
Together we travel this river of fervid stars.

## Before the Wall

Tonight with the blade's weight
of spackle I obscure
gouges mute chairs made
those nights when smoky windows
choked your dreams
Messages from one accused
live in lightning
ripple toward the freezer

Under long rolls
of thunder I cover them
with ease

2 a.m. orgies of earlier tenants
still show through

**297**

His madman's dent
Her cloying repartee
while poisoning their food
the way they left a trail of ashes
nodding like outgoing sails
I've covered them with foothills

with enough snow
to silence
even their relatives

4 a.m. I'm plastering
waves to ride toward your return
In dim light I reach
the first star you saw
in the Sangre de Christos.
I recognize these strains of seaweed
now    Come home    Someone is trying
to lead me astray before
I can claim them


## Departure's Girlfriend

He drove her to wander over sand
that solid excitement of the sea's great churning
to sniff the bitter nooks of horse chestnuts
to hesitate before the pink brown eyes of moths
to revel in the company of weeds
spilling their clarity into snow

He claimed her kin to oak groves
and illuminated the silk dark creeks
with gold flecks of her solitude
until she sought the warmth
of wooden porches

He dreamed her umber in moonlight
and had her count
faces of those forgotten

in wands of ocher willows
in the drifting ash of an autumn fire

He rooted her flesh
in sienna in the brilliant brown dance
of ordinary beings      Now she knows
who will hesitate
and who will go into the mountains
when time drops its radiance down

He told her
to rise from obedience
and bless the bare trees whenever they kiss
an empty horizon

She stretched inward and outward at once
expecting her dark face
to fade
down every aisle
while clerks continue counting
their spare change

# Jonathan Williams

## Farmer Beresford, on Nobility in Langstrothdale Chase

if thou piss free,
fart dry,
and pay 20 shillings in t' pound,

no man can touch thee!


## Shepherd

I could tell he were gone,
his eye were cold

just like when you tell a dead lamb's,
it were like that


## A.L.B. (1917–1978)

he was
oald as the fells,
street as an arske's arse,
sharp as whins,
whick as a lop,
wild as winter thunner,
nice as an otter

and his throat war middlen slippy,
and he is deed as a steann . . .

but not gone
but not gone

## A Ride in a Blue Chevy from Alum Cave Trail to Newfound Gap

goin' hikin'?
git in!

o the Smokies are ok but me
i go for Theosophy,
higher things, Hindu-type philosophy,
none of this licker and sex, i
like it
on what we call the astral plane,
i reckon i get more i-thridral
by the hour!

buddy, you won't believe this but
how old you reckon the earth is?
the earth is
precisely 156 trillion years old—
i got this book from headquarters in
Wheaton, Illinois
says it is!

i'll tell you somethin' else:
there are exactly 144 kinds of people on this earth—
12 signs and the signs change
every two hours,
that's 144, i'm Scorpio,
with Mars over the water . . .

here's somethin' else innerrestin':
back 18 million years
people was only one sex, one sex only—
i'd like to explain that,
it's right here in this pamphlet:
50 cents . . .

never married, lived with my mother in Ohio,
she died, i'm over in Oak Ridge
in a machine shop, say,
what kind of place

is Denver?
think i'll sell this car, go to Denver,
set up a Center . . .

name's Davis,
what's yours?


## The Fourteen-Year-Old Samuel Palmer's Watercolor Notations for the Sketch "A Lane at Thanet":

grey sky
mottled with blue &
warmish light

this thatch
very bright

elder
berry very bright

this
little
gate

very bright

br. light

# Nellie Wong

## Moving to Her New House

*Written on the day my sister, Leslie Jow, left this world,*
*January 16, 1985.*

"This dining table will be great," she says,
"it's old, it's mahogany, and look, how many leaves!
We'll be able to have the whole family over for dinner."

And she sprays the windows with Windex,
makes them shine. Outside the trees shade
the huge living room.

She spreads Chinese rugs on the hardwood floors,
puts vases of fresh chrysanthemums, Father's favorite,
everywhere: in the kitchen, bedrooms and bath.

The house prepares for her arrival.
Its wings expand and escort her inside.
Her eyes widen. And she still plans
to visit China, the ancestral village of her parents.

She wears her niece's crocheted hat
to keep her head warm. She bundles up
in her husband's gift of a Christmas jacket.
Diamond earrings sparkle from her earlobes.
What a special occasion. Moving to her new house!
Where nephew Sam will play with Dennis
and eat *loh bock goh* and the family's laughter
at "Trivial Pursuit" will ring throughout the house.

The oil in the wok sizzles. The oven's on.
There'll be chow mein, roast duck, ratatouille,

and fresh morning buns and the feasting will spread
in a new house on a quiet hill on Spruce Street.

Ring the bell! Gather the oranges and sweetmeats!
Leslie's moving to her new house!


## We Go as American Tourists

Ferrying toward Nanaimo
we breathe the salt air of Vancouver Bay.
We go inland, wind into Chinatown.
Wooden shacks, closed stores, western
as the backlot of a Hollywood film studio.
An old man approaches,
invites us for coffee in his tiny store.
He tells us: not much here,
only the old, the very, very young.
The children have moved away.
Narrowing toward us, an old woman,
a small boy. We aim our cameras,
focusing on what blossoms
as an old China scene.
We close in. Folding the boy into
her long black skirt, the woman flees
the distance of our Chinese faces,
the shapely ghosts of our western clothes.

# Ray A. Young Bear

## The Dream of Purple Birds in Marshall, Washington

My people back home love purple—
on clothes for ceremonial or everyday wear.
But the two birds who reside near the city
of Spokane, like us, wear this color as well.
On morning two, they flutter and tap
their purple bodies against our window.
They attempt to tell us something.
Or as I dread, as I have felt
through sleeplessness,
they are the once-life of two women
whose body parts lie scattered
and hidden safely under the dirt and rocks
of a railroad track—
the same one that winds through
this community, this pinetree-lined
valley. In desperation I ask one bird,
"Ka da shai? What is wrong with you?"
With its purple mask and cape, the bird
hopped on a branch and turned more towards
my way as further testament:
the underside of its body was white-colored
with red speckled lines flowing from its neck
to its chest. These innocent ladies are here
somewhere, they tell me, beckoning you
from dream, from Iowa, from yourself.
Tonight, to keep all this away from me,
I will apply a thin, transparent coat
of yellow paint over the top half
of my round face: *I refuse to be*
*their spiritual conduit and release*
*in a valley where the sun darkens early,*
*in a valley where a large, red fluorescent*
*cross is physically so much stronger*
*than I . . .*

305

# Three Translated Poems for October

Old woman, I hope that at least
you will watch me in the future
when I am an elderly man—
so my baggy clothes
do not catch fire
when I socialize
with the young people
as they stand around
the campfire intoxicated.
Of course, I will tell them
worldly things.

         \*    \*    \*

Now that the autumn season
has started, one suddenly
realizes the act of living
goes fast.
Sometimes the spring
is that way, too:
the green so quick.
Thirty-two years of age I am.
Box elder leaves are being shaken
by the cold rain and wind.
In the tree's nakedness
there stands a man,
visible.

         \*    \*    \*

Although there is yet
alot of things to do,
surprisingly, I have this urge
to go fishing.
They say the whites
in town will pay
one hundred dollars
to whoever catches
the largest channel catfish
or flathead.
You know I like to fish.

We could invite and feed
lots of friends.
Plus, purchase
a cast iron woodstove
since the business committee
has ignored our weatherization
application, but Bingo
is on the agenda.

# *Yvonne*

---

## From *Iwilla/Scourge*

Evangeline

1

your new shoes click and slide upon the floor
a floor of many colors like your brother's marbles
what is that smell?     a birthday smell?
but cool and dim like the cellar
murmurs swim somewhere above your head
like the radio sighing in your mother's bedroom
grownup talk, conspiracy
a voice stands behind you
a motherly voice with her brown hand upon your shoulder
it is not your mother's hand
*what is your name?*
he has a thin mouth in a thin red face
his hair is thick and white
he is not a doctor because you are not sick
and he wears a purple dress
*what do you ask of the Church of God?*
your mother stands near but she does not speak
your brothers lurk in the darkness of the cool huge stones
your dress is white and the lace scratches your neck
the strange man gives you salt
he waves his hand before you many times
but he does not leave     you cannot leave
the strange brown hand upon your shoulder
he puts his hand upon your forehead
is he looking for fever?
you are not sick
*do you renounce Satan all his works all his allurements?*
he does not frown like a doctor

he is not brown like a father
your father in the great book of pictures at home
*do you believe?*
the lace scratches your neck but this is a pretty dress
like a party dress but this is not a party
but can't you smell the candles?
somewhere above your head
and he gives you
but where are the other children?
your brothers stand in the dark
*receive this white garment*
*receive this burning candle*

. . . . . . . . . . . . .


5


before you know the years are lost
somewhere down the wooden porch stairs
where your brothers disappear and can hardly be heard
above what must be the girls next door
*here we go zoodeeo zoodeeo zoodeeo*
*here we go zoodeeo all day long*
you learn all the words
and hunger for the curve of every voice
as you sit among serious shoes
of Aunt Corinna and Aunt Ida who linger after church
because your mother is alone
long before you know that she is alone
sometimes they applaud your sweet singing to your dolls
*the child takes the nurse the nurse takes the dog*
but they never join you down on the scratchy porch rug
the way your mother does
but then you do not remember when she disappears
behind the screen door at the top of the stairs
and you are standing at the edge
your heart a perfect swoop and soar
of the game the big girls play
but the big girls never believe you
although you never know this for many years
because they smile and close their hands and do not let

you escape from their strong brown circle
*red rover     red rover     I call Evangeline over*
now you are redlightgreenlight quick
now you are polite     *mother may I? take two giant steps*
*backwards     yes you may*
no they never believe
*engine engine # 9 going down Chicago line*
you arrive too late
*if the train goes off the track do you want your*
*money back?*     and leave too soon
you pick up all the sticks
you pick up all the jacks one by one
you are a safety-first player     you are a gambler
but you do not know
all these years when your opponent is unknown
*the cheese stands alone*


## 6

sit down
all-American oak
double desks single desks
nailed down in rows
before heavy huge infallible desk
before immutable black veil
black gown against black chalkboard
crucifix nailed above
stand and pray     stand and pledge
sit down
hear listen see believe question answer
memorizememorizememorize
boys in front (cannot be trusted)
girls in back (must not tempt)
and in places of honor
last desk every row
you (always the only "only")
and other really smart girls
sit down
you you really smart girls
hope to be correct to be asked

what do you know what do you remember?
hope to please and be suitable
(competere, in Latin: to come together
to agree, to be suitable
in English: to compete, to vie
as if for a prize) you you
really smart girl with five talents
(give back ten) with ten talents
(give back twenty) only one talent?
what do you mean? retarded? are you poor?
pagan baby in Asia? colored girl in the South?
how dare you hide behind desks in front
stand up    clap erasers    wash boards    hand out
papers scissors    writewritewrite
your hands fall off    thisisatest    grade tests
police when the nun leaves the room
or be cast out into utter darkness    yes
yes    *Evangeline you are colored and a credit*
*stand up*    in the footsteps of Eve

# Bibliography of Publishers, Journals, and Anthologies

The following is a list of presses, magazines, and anthologies in which the work of American poets can be found. Because some of the work may be difficult to locate through conventional channels, we have included addresses so that material can be ordered directly from the presses. In addition, we have mentioned a number of anthologies and collections. Some of the titles are our choices, others have been culled from *The International Directory of Little Magazines and Small Presses*, edited by Len Fulton and Ellen Ferber. (This very useful volume can be ordered directly from Dustbooks, P.O. Box 100, Paradise, CA 95969. It is updated periodically.) Names and addresses of small presses publishing our contributors are also included.

Many university presses emphasize the work of writers within their region. Among them are the University of Arizona Press, the University of New Mexico Press, the University of Indiana Press, the University of Pittsburgh Press, and the Navajo Community College Press. We would advise the reader to examine the university and community college lists for relevant texts. And, of course, bookstores that specialize in poetry can be an invaluable resource.

For the time being, anyone interested in locating the works of the full spectrum of American poets must see the task as a search. We can only hope that the reader will find the process enlightening and the results exciting.

## Presses and Journals

*Afro-Hispanic Review.* Romance Languages, University of Missouri, Columbia, MO 65211.

*Akwekon: A National Native American Literature and Arts Journal.* Akwesane Notes, P.O. Box 223, Hogansburg, NY 13655.

Alice James Books, 33 Richdale Avenue, Cambridge, MA 02140.

*American Book Review*. P.O. Box 188, Cooper Station, New York, NY 10003 (includes reviews of books from small, regional, Third World, and women's presses).

*Appalachian Heritage*. Hutchins Library, Berea College, Berea, KY 40404.

*Appalachian Journal*. Appalachian Consortium Press, University Hall, Appalachian State University, Boone, NC 28607.

Arte Público Press, University of Houston, University Park, Houston, TX 77004 (Hispanic literature).

*Aztlán: International Journal of Chicano Studies Research*. Chicano Studies Research Center Publications, UCLA, 405 Hilgard Avenue, Los Angeles, CA 90025.

*Backbone*. P.O. Box 95315, Seattle, WA 98145 (women writers with diverse economic, cultural, stylistic views).

*Bamboo Ridge: The Hawaii Writers Quarterly*. Bamboo Ridge Press, P.O. Box 61781, Honolulu, HI 96822-8781.

Bear Tribe Publishing, P.O. Box 9167, Spokane, WA 99209.

*Belles Lettres*. P.O. Box 987, Arlington, VA 22216 (review of books by women).

*Bilingual Review*. Bilingual Press, Hispanic Research Center, Arizona State University, Tempe, AZ 85287.

*Black American Literature Forum*. Indiana State University, Parsons Hall 237, Terre Haute, IN 47809.

*Black Maria*. Metis Press, Inc., P.O. Box 25187, Chicago, IL 60625 (material by and about women).

Black Oyster Press, P.O. Box 8550, Chicago, IL 60680 (feminist).

Black River Writers Press, P.O. Box 6165, East St. Louis, IL 62202.

*The Black Scholar: Journal of Black Studies and Research*. The Black Scholar Press, P.O. Box 7106, San Francisco, CA 94120.

*Blackberry*. Chimney Farm, RR1, Box 228, Nobelboro, ME 04555 (special interest in Native American work).

*Blue Cloud Quarterly*. Blue Cloud Abbey, Box 98, Marvin, SD 57251 (poetry by Native Americans).

*Boletín Anglohispano*. Bola Publications, 2378 Willowbrae Drive, Eagle Pass, TX 78852-3870.

*Bridge: Asian American Perspectives*. 32 E. Broadway, New York, NY 10002.

*Callaloo*. Department of English, University of Virginia, Charlottesville, VA 22903 (creative literature by black writers and critical works about black literature).

Callaloo Poetry Series, Department of English, University of Kentucky, Lexington, KY 40506.

*Calyx: A Journal of Art and Literature by Women*. Calyx Books, P.O. Box B, Corvallis, OR 97339.

*Carta Abierta*. Relampago Books Press, Center for Mexican-American Studies, Texas Lutheran College, Sequin, TX 78155.

Cinco Puntos Press, 2709 Louisville, El Paso, TX 79930 (literature of the Southwest).

Clothespin Fever Press, 5529 N. Figueroa, Los Angeles, CA 90042 (lesbian).

*Common Lives/Lesbian Lives.* P.O. Box 1553, Iowa City, IA 52244.

*Conditions.* P.O. Box 56, Van Brunt Station, Brooklyn, NY 11215 (feminist with emphasis on writing by lesbians).

*Contact/II: A Bimonthly Poetry Review Magazine.* Contact II Publications, P.O. Box 451, Bowling Green Station, New York, NY 10004 (multicultural, special issue—*Asian American: North and South,* vol. 7, no. 38/39/40 [Winter/Spring 1986]).

Cordillera, 4 Marshall Road, Natick, MA 01760 (press that publishes many minority writers).

*Coyote's Journal.* P.O. Box 629, Brunswick, ME 04011.

Crones' Own Press, 814 Demerius Street, R-2, Durham, NC 27701-1629 (publishes mid-life and older women).

The Crossing Press, P.O. Box 1048, Freedom, CA 95019-1048 (multicultural list).

The David Company, P.O. Box 19355, Chicago, IL 60619.

*Day Tonight/Night Today.* P.O. Box 353, Hull, MA 02045 (women).

*Empire! The NYS Inmate Literary Arts Magazine.* Arthur Kill Correctional Facility, 2911 Arthur Kill Road, Staten Island, NY 10309.

*The Evergreen Chronicles.* P.O. Box 6260, Minnehaha Station, Minneapolis, MN 55406 (gay/lesbian, Midwest).

*Exquisite Corpse: A Monthly of Books and Ideas.* English Department, Louisiana State University, Baton Rouge, LA 70803-50001 (eclectic—poetry, articles, reviews, criticism).

*Fag Rag.* Good Gay Poets Press. Fag Rag Collective, Box 331, Kenmore Station, Boston, MA 02215.

*Fastbook Series.* Plain View Press, Inc., 1509 Dexter, Austin, TX 78704 (emphasizes work by women).

*Feminist Studies.* c/o Women's Studies Program, University of Maryland, College Park, MD 20742.

Firebrand Books, 141 The Commons, Ithaca, NY 14850 (feminist and lesbian).

*Frontiers: A Journal of Women's Studies.* c/o Women's Studies, Campus Box 325, University of Colorado, Boulder, CO 80309.

*Gay Chicago Magazine.* 1527 N. Wells Street, Chicago, IL 60610.

Gay Presses of New York, P.O. Box 294, Village Station, New York, NY 10014.

Greenfield Review Press, Ithaca House, RD 1, Box 80, Greenfield Center, NY 12833 (multicultural and innovative list).

*Hanging Loose.* Hanging Loose Press, 231 Wyckoff Street, Brooklyn, NY 11217 (includes many gay, feminist, Third World poets; *Hanging Loose* 52 has a Latino supplement).

*Helicon Nine: The Journal of Women's Arts and Letters.* P.O. Box 22412, Kansas City, MO 64113.

HerBooks, P.O. Box 7467, Santa Cruz, CA 95061 (lesbian feminist).

*Heresies: A Feminist Publication on Art and Politics.* Box 1306, Canal Street Station, New York, NY 10013.

*How(Ever)*. How(ever) Press, 554 Jersey Street, San Francisco, CA 94114 (women's experimental poetry).

*Hurricane Alice*. 207 Church Street SE, Minneapolis, MN 55455 (feminist literature and art).

*Ikon*. Ikon Press, P.O. Box 1355, Stuyvesant Station, New York, NY 10009 (feminist political, cultural magazine with writing by lesbian, Third World, and working-class women).

*Imagine: International Chicano Poetry Journal*. Imagine Publishers, Inc., 89 Massachusetts Avenue, Suite 270, Boston, MA 02115.

*Iowa Woman*. P.O. Box 680, Iowa City, IA 52244 (midwestern women).

I. Reed Books, 285 E. Third Avenue, New York, NY 10009.

*James White Review: A Gay Men's Literary Quarterly*. P.O. Box 3356, Traffic Station, Minneapolis, MN 55403.

Juniper Press, 1310 Sherwood Drive, La Crosse, WI 54601.

*Kalliope, A Journal of Women's Art*. 3939 Roosevelt Boulevard, Florida Community College at Jacksonville, Jacksonville, FL 32205.

Kelsey St. Press, P.O. Box 9235, Berkeley, CA 94709.

Kitchen Table: Women of Color Press, P.O. Box 908, Latham, NY 12110-0908.

*Latin American Literary Review*. Latin American Literary Review Press, Department of Hispanic Language and Literature, 1309 Cathedral of Learning, University of Pittsburgh, Pittsburgh, PA 15260.

*Lector*. California Spanish Language Data Base, P.O. Box 4273, Berkeley, CA 94704 (Hispanic-related material).

*Longhouse*. Green River, Jacksonville Stage, Brattleboro, VT 05301.

Lotus Press, Inc., P.O. Box 21607, Detroit, MI 48221 (emphasis on black poets).

Magic Circle Press, 10 Hyde Ridge Road, Weston, CT 06833 (has done special project on poetry of women in prison).

Maize Press, 961 Bakersfield, Pismo Beach, CA 93449 (poetry chapbooks).

*Mati*. Omnation Press, 5548 N. Sawyer, Chicago, IL 60625 (interested in experimental poetry, especially by women).

Mina Press, P.O. Box 854, Sebastpol, CA 95472 (previously unpublished and non-mainstream writers).

Minor Heron Press, P.O. Box 2615, Taos, NM 87571 (emphasis on Southwestern Hispanic and Native American poetry and fiction).

*Motheroot Journal*. Motheroot Publications, P.O. Box 8306, Pittsburgh, PA 15218-0306 (women's press; the journal reviews small press books by or about women).

*Moving Out: Feminist Literary and Arts Journal*. P.O. Box 21249, Detroit, MI 48221.

*New Sins*. P.O. Box A-3597, Chicago, IL 60690 (gay and lesbian poetry).

New Victoria Publishers, P.O. Box 27, Norwich, VT 05055 (women's press).

*Notebook: A Little Magazine*. Esoterica Press, P.O. Box B-43, Los Angeles, CA 90026 (first issue devoted to writing by Chicanos and Latinos; Asian, Native American, black, Arab American encouraged to submit).

*Now and Then*. P.O. Box 19, 180A, East Tennessee State University, Johnson City, TN 37614-0002 (a publication of the Institute for Appalachian Studies and Services of East Tennessee University).

*Parnassus: Poetry in Review*. 41 Union Square West, Room 804, New York, NY 10024.

Pentagon Press, Box 379, Markesan, WI 53946.

Poetessa Press, P.O. Box 420, East Rockaway, NY 11518 (women).

*Primavera*. 1212 East 59th Street, Chicago, IL 60637 (feminist).

*The Redneck Review of Literature*. Route 1, Box 1085, Fairfield, ID 83327 (literature of West; seeks Native American work).

Sea Horse Press, 307 W. 11th Street, New York, NY 10014 (gay prose and poetry).

Seal Press, 3131 Western Avenue, Suite 410, Seattle, WA 98121-1028 (feminist).

Seven Buffaloes Press, Box 249, Big Timber, MT 59011 (publishes *Black Jack* and *Valley Grapevine*, which focus on regional and rural writing).

*Sez: A Multi-Racial Journal of Poetry and People's Culture*. Shadow Press, P.O. Box 8803, Minneapolis, MN 55408.

Shamal Books, G.P.O. Box 16, New York, NY 10016 (multicultural list).

Shameless Hussy Press, P.O. Box 5540, Berkeley, CA 94705.

*Signs: Journal of Women in Culture and Society*. Women's Studies Research Center, 207 East Duke Building, Durham, NC 27708.

*Sing Heavenly Muse!: Women's Poetry and Prose*. P.O. Box 13299, Minneapolis, MN 55414.

*Sinister Wisdom*. P.O. Box 3252, Berkeley, CA 94703 (feminist, lesbian, multicultural).

Sinister Wisdom Books, P.O. Box 1308, Montpelier, VT 05602 (feminist, lesbian).

*So & So*. Dragon Cloud Books, As Is/So & So Press, 123 N. 8th Avenue, Highland Park, NJ 08904 (multicultural).

South End Press, 116 St. Botolph Street, Boston, MA 02115 (books that aid the day-to-day struggle to control life).

*Southern Exposure*. Institute for Southern Studies, P.O. Box 531, Durham, NC 27702.

*Spinsters/Aunt Lute*, P.O. Box 410687, San Francisco, CA 94141 (books and art work by women).

*Steppingstones: A Literary Anthology Toward Liberation*. Steppingstones Press, Box 1856, New York, NY 10027 (especially Third World and black).

Strawberry Press, P.O. Box 451, Bowling Green Station, New York, NY 10004 (Native American).

*Telewoman*. Telewoman Inc., P.O. Box 2306, Pleasant Hill, CA 94523 (lesbian).

*Third Woman*. Third Woman Press, c/o Chicano Studies, Dwinelle Hall 3404, University of California at Berkeley, Berkeley, CA 94720.

*Thirteenth Moon*. P.O. Box 309, Cathedral Station, New York, NY 10025 (particularly interested in feminist and lesbian work; vol. 7, nos. 1 and 2, is a double issue on working-class experience).

*Tulsa Studies in Women's Literature*. 600 S. College, Tulsa, OK 74104.

*The Universal Black Writer.* P.O. Box 5, Radio City Station, New York, NY 10101.

*Valley Women's Voice.* 40 Every Woman's Center, Wilder Hall, University of Massachusetts, Amherst, MA 01003.

*Viaztlán: A Journal of Arts and Letters.* Centro Cultural Aztlán, 211 South Pecos Street #239, San Antonio, TX 78207-4040 (Hispanic literature and arts).

*Voices.* Etana-Ebra Press, P.O. Box 20525, Wichita, KS 67208 (poetry, writers who are not widely published, working class, black, women, Midwest).

Waterfront Press, 52 Maple Avenue, Maplewood, NJ 07040 (specializes in work by Puerto Rican and other Hispanic writers).

West End Press, P.O. Box 27334, Albuquerque, NM 87125 (politically progressive).

White Pine Press, 76 Center Street, Fredonia, NY 14063.

*Woman Poet.* Women-in-Literature, Inc., P.O. Box 60550, Reno, NV 89506.

*Women's Compendium.* P.O. Box 1651, Modesto, CA 95353.

*Women's Quarterly Review.* P.O. Box 708, New York, NY 10150.

*The Women's Review of Books.* Wellesley College, Center for Research on Women, Wellesley, MA 02181.

*Women's Studies Quarterly.* The Feminist Press at the City University of New York, 311 East 94th Street, New York, NY 10128.

## Anthologies

Algarin, Miguel, and Miguel Piñero, eds. *Nuyorican Poetry: An Anthology of Puerto Rican Words and Feelings.* New York: William Morrow and Co., 1975.

Allen, Terry, ed. *The Whispering Wind: Poetry by Young American Indians.* New York: Doubleday, 1972.

Amburgey, Gail, Mary Joan Coleman, and Pauletta Hansel, eds. *We're Alright but We Ain't Special.* Beckley, W. Va.: Mountain Union Books, 1976.

Astrov, Margot, ed. *American Indian Prose and Poetry.* New York: Capricorn Books, 1946.

Baber, Bob Henry, George Ella Lyon, and Gurney Norman, eds. *Common Ground: Contemporary Appalachian Poetry.* Charleston, W. Va.: Jalamap Press, 1985.

Bambara, Toni Cade, ed. *The Black Woman: An Anthology.* New York: New American Library, 1970.

Baraka, Amiri, and Amina Baraka, eds. *Confirmation: An Anthology of African-American Women.* New York: Quill, 1983.

Barradas, Efraín, and Rafael Rodríguez, eds. *Herejes y mitificadores: Muestra de poesía puertorriqueña en los Estados Unidos.* Puerto Rico: Ediciones Huracán, 1980 (bilingual).

Bernikow, Louise, ed. *The World Split Open: Four Centuries of Women Poets in England and America, 1552–1950.* New York: Vintage, 1974.

Bierhorst, John, ed. *In the Trail of the Wind.* New York: Farrar, Straus and Giroux, 1971.

Bly, Robert, ed. *News of the Universe: Poems of Twofold Consciousness.* San Francisco, Calif.: Sierra Club Books, 1980.

Brant, Beth, ed. *A Gathering of Spirit: Writing and Art by North American Indian Women*. Rockland, Maine: Sinister Wisdom Books, 1984.

Bruchac, Joseph, ed. *Breaking Silence: An Anthology of Contemporary Asian American Poets*. Greenfield Center, N.Y.: Greenfield Review Press, 1983.

————. *The Light from Another Country: Poetry from American Prisons*. Greenfield Center, N.Y.: Greenfield Review Press, 1984.

————. *Songs from This Earth on Turtle's Back: Contemporary American Indian Poetry*. Greenfield Center, N.Y.: Greenfield Review Press, 1983.

Bulkin, Elly, and Joan Larkin, eds. *Lesbian Poetry: An Anthology*. Watertown, Mass.: Persephone, 1981 (distributed by Gay Presses of New York).

Chapman, Abraham, ed. *Literature of the American Indians*. New York: Meridian, 1975.

Chiang, Fay et al., eds. *American Born and Foreign*. New York: Sunbury, 1979.

Delgado, Abelardo, ed. *Chicano: Twenty-five Pieces of a Chicano Mind*. Denver: Barrio Publications, 1969.

Epringham, Toni, ed. *Fiesta in Aztlán*. Santa Barbara, Calif.: Capra Press, 1981.

Fisher, Dexter, ed. *The Third Woman: Minority Women Writers of the United States*. Boston, Mass.: Houghton Mifflin, 1980.

Frumkin, Gene, and Stanley Noyes, eds. *The Indian Rio Grande: Recent Poems from Three Cultures*. Albuquerque, N.M.: San Marcos Press, 1977.

Gibson, Donald B., ed. *Modern Black Poets*. Englewood Cliffs, N.J.: Prentice-Hall, 1973.

Green, Rayna, ed. *That's What She Said: Contemporary Poetry and Fiction by Native American Women*. Bloomington, Ind.: Indiana University Press, 1984.

Henderson, Stephen. *Understanding the New Black Poetry*. New York: William Morrow and Co., 1973.

Hicks, Granville, et al., eds. *Proletarian Literature in the United States: An Anthology*. New York: International Publishers, 1935.

Hobson, Geary, ed. *The Remembered Earth: An Anthology of Contemporary Native American Literature*. Albuquerque, N.M.: University of New Mexico Press, 1981.

Howe, Florence, and Ellen Bass, eds. *No More Masks! An Anthology of Poems by Women*. New York: Doubleday Anchor, 1973.

Japanese American Anthology Committee, ed. *Ayumi: A Japanese American Anthology*. P.O. Box 5024, San Francisco, CA, 1980.

Katz, Janet, ed. *I Am the Fire of Time: Writings by Native American Women*. New York: Dutton, 1977.

Keller, Gary, and Francisco Jimenez. *Hispanics in the United States: An Anthology of Creative Literature*. Tempe, Ariz.: Bilingual Press, Arizona State University, 1980 (vol. 1), 1982 (vol. 2).

Kenny, Maurice, ed. *Wounds Beneath the Flesh: Fifteen Native American Poets*. Marvin, S. Dak.: Blue Cloud Quarterly Press, 1983.

Kherdian, David, ed. *Settling America: The Ethnic Expression of Fourteen Contemporary Poets*. New York: Macmillan, 1974.

Kowit, Steve, ed. *The Maverick Poets*. Gorilla Press, 9269 Mission Gorge Road, Suite 229, Santee, CA 92071.

**319**

Kuzma, Greg, ed. *Alternatives*. Lincoln, Neb.: Best Cellar Press, 1987.

Leyland, Winston, ed. *Orgasms of Light: The Gay Sunshine Anthology*. San Francisco, Calif.: Gay Sunshine Press, 1977.

Lourie, Dick, ed. *Come to Power: Eleven Contemporary American Indian Poets*. Freedom, N.Y.: Crossing Press, 1974.

Lowenfels, Walter, ed. *From the Belly of the Shark*. New York: Vintage, 1973.

Marzán, Julio, ed. *Inventing a Word: An Anthology of Twentieth-Century Puerto Rican Poetry*. New York: Columbia University Press, 1980.

Matila, Alfredo, and Iván Silén, eds. *The Puerto Rican Poets*. New York: Bantam, 1972.

Miles, Sara, et al., eds. *Ordinary Women, Mujeres Comunes: An Anthology of Poetry by New York City Women*. New York: Ordinary Women, 1978.

Moraga, Cherríe, and Gloria Anzaldúa, eds. *This Bridge Called My Back: Writings by Radical Women of Color*. Watertown, Mass.: Persephone Press, 1981 (distributed by Kitchen Table: Women of Color Press).

Morse, Carl, and Joan Larkin, eds. *Gay and Lesbian Poets in Our Time: An Anthology*. New York: St. Martin's Press, 1988.

Niatum, Duane, ed. *Carriers of the Dream Wheel: Contemporary Native American Poetry*. New York: Harper and Row, 1975.

————. *Harper's Anthology of Twentieth-Century Native American Poetry*. New York: Harper and Row, 1987.

North, Joseph, ed. *New Masses: An Anthology of the Rebel Thirties*. New York: International Publishers, 1969.

Piercy, Marge, ed. *Early Ripening: American Women's Poetry Now*. New York: Pandora Press, 1987.

Randall, Dudley, ed. *The Black Poets*. New York: Bantam Books, 1971.

Simon, Myron, ed. *Ethnic Writers in America*. New York: Harcourt Brace Jovanovich, 1972.

Steiner, Stan, and Luis Valdez, eds. *Aztlán: An Anthology of Mexican American Literature*. New York: Random House, 1972.

Stetson, Arlene, ed. *Black Sister: Poetry by Black American Women, 1746–1980*. Bloomington: Indiana University Press, 1981.

Troupe, Quincy, and Rainer Schulte, eds. *Giant Talk: An Anthology of Third World Writing*. New York: Random House, 1975.

Young, Ian, ed. *The Male Muse: A Gay Anthology*. Freedom, Calif.: Crossing Press, 1973.

————. *Son of the Male Muse: New Gay Poetry*. Freedom, Calif.: Crossing Press, 1983.

# Contributors

*Steve Abbott* published *Soup* magazine from 1980–84 and has edited *Poetry Flash* since 1979. Besides writing frequent art criticism for *The Advocate* and other magazines, he has published four books, the most recent *Lives of the Poets* (Black Star Series, 1987). He teaches writing at the University of San Francisco.

*Paula Gunn Allen* is of Laguna Pueblo-Sioux-Scottish-American and Lebanese American descent. She is a professor of ethnic and Native American studies at the University of California, Berkeley. In 1978 she received a fellowship from the National Endowment for the Arts and in 1984 was appointed Associate Fellow for Humanities at Stanford University. She is the author of four chapbooks and two books of poetry, the most recent *Wyrds* (Taurean Horn Press, 1987). Her essays are collected in *The Sacred Hoop: Recovering the Feminine in American Indian Traditions* (Beacon Press, 1986).

*Alurista* has published six collections of poetry. He is an assistant professor of Spanish at California Polytechnic State University, San Luis Obispo, and a distinguished visiting lecturer in Chicano studies at the University of California, Santa Barbara. He is West Coast editor for the literary and academic journals *Confluencia*, *Imagine*, and *ViAztlán*. His most recent collection is *Return* (Bilingual Review Press, 1982).

*Maggie Anderson* is the author of three collections of poems, the most recent *Cold Comfort* (University of Pittsburgh Press, 1986). She has received fellowships from the National Endowment for the Arts, the Pennsylvania Council on the Arts, and the West Virginia Arts and Humanities Commission. She has taught in the writing programs at the University of Pittsburgh and Pennsylvania State University, and is currently writer in residence at the University of Oregon.

321

*Antler* is a Great Lakes Bioregion poet whose books include *Factory* (City Lights) and *Last Words* (Ballantine). He is the 1985 winner of the Walt Whitman Prize and the 1987 winner of the Witter Bynner Prize for Poetry awarded by the American Academy and Institute of Arts and Letters.

*Bob Arnold* is a stonemason in Vermont and editor of *Longhouse*, an independent magazine in its fifteenth year of publication. He is the author of twelve books, the most recent *Where Rivers Meet* (Juniper Press, 1988).

*Russell Atkins* is a poet and composer who edited the magazine *Free Lance* from 1950 to 1980. He holds an honorary doctorate from Cleveland State University, an Ohio Arts Council Fellowship, and is a consultant for Cleveland Educational Television. He has published four chapbooks, including *Here in The* (Cleveland State University Poetry Center Press, 1976).

*Bob Henry Baber* is the inventor of the "lowku," a new American form of poetry that must be less than seventeen syllables. He is program director of Appalshop, Inc. Teacher, editor, writer-in-residence, he is a founding member of the Soupbean Poets of Antioch/Appalachia. His fourth book of poetry is *Ice Sicle Soup* (West Virginia Tech, 1986).

*Jimmy Santiago Baca* is a full-time poet whose two most recent books are *Martin* (New Directions, 1987) and *Poems Taken from My Yard* (Timberline Press, 1986). He is a recipient of a fellowship from the National Endowment for the Arts.

*Robin Becker* serves as poetry editor for *The Women's Review of Books* and is the recipient of numerous residency grants and a fellowship, in 1985, from the Massachusetts Artists Foundation. She was an assistant professor in the Writing Program at Massachusetts Institute of Technology. Her collection of poetry, *Backtalk*, was published in 1982 by Alice James Books.

*Duane Big Eagle* belongs to the Osage Tribe. He is editor and publisher of Ten Mile River Press and works in the California Poets-in-the-Schools Program.

*Karen Brodine* worked as a typesetter, writing teacher, and editor. Her work was widely published in the feminist, left, and gay/lesbian press. She was a founding member of the Women Writers Union in the Bay Area and a member of Radical Women and the Freedom Socialist Party. Her only book, *Illegal Assembly*, is available from Hanging Loose Press. She died of cancer in 1987.

*Gwendolyn Brooks* is Poet Laureate of Illinois and a member of the American Academy and Institute of Arts and Letters. Among her awards are the Pulitzer Prize for Poetry, the Shelly Memorial Award, the Kuumba Liberation Award, and two Guggenheim fellowships. She is the author of fifteen books, has edited two anthologies, and has read her poetry throughout the United States, Europe, and Africa.

*Joseph Bruchac* is of Slovak and Abenaki heritage. He is the author of twelve books of poetry, the most recent of which is *Near the Mountains* (White Pine Press, 1987). He is the founding editor, with his wife, Carol, of the *Greenfield Review* (1969–87) and the Greenfield Review Press, for which he has edited, among other anthologies, *The Light from Another Country: Poetry from American Prisons* (1984) and *Songs from This Earth on Turtle's Back: Contemporary American Indian Poetry* (1983).

*David Budbill* is the creator of the fictional rural New England town of Judevine, the inhabitants of which people his poems and stories and plays. His most recent book of poetry is *Why I Came to Judevine* (White Pine Press, 1987).

*Jo Carson* is a poet, playwright, fiction writer, and occasional commentator for National Public Radio's "All Things Considered." She is the poetry editor of *Now & Then*, a magazine published by the Center for Appalachian Studies and Services. Her collection of poetry is *Stories I Ain't Told Nobody Yet* (Appalachian Consortium Press).

*Ana Castillo* is a novelist and poet whose books of poems include *Women Are Not Roses* (Arte Público Press, 1984) and *My Father Was a Toltec* (West End Press, 1988). Her novels are *The Mixquiahuala Letters* (1986) and *Sapognoia* (1988), both published by Bilingual Press. She is an associate editor and reviewer for *Third Woman Magazine* and coeditor of *Humanizarte*, as well as a freelance writer and lecturer.

*Lorna Dee Cervantes* was editor/publisher/printer of Mango Publications. She was the recipient, in 1978, of a fellowship from the National Endowment for the Arts. Her work has appeared in many journals and has been anthologized in *The Third Woman*. Her first volume of poems is *Emplumada* (University of Pittsburgh Press, 1981).

*Lillie D. Chaffin* has published poetry and fiction, juvenile literature and an autobiography. Her *Eighth Day Thirteenth Moon* (Pikeville College Press) was nominated for the Pulitzer Prize.

*Diana Chang* is the author of six novels. Her first collection of poems, *The Horizon Is Definitely Speaking*, was published by Backstreet Editions of Street Press. Her second book of poetry and drawings, *What Matisse Is After*, was published by Contact II in 1984. She is a painter and teaches creative writing at Barnard College.

*Sandra Cisneros* teaches at California State University, Chico. Her book of fiction, *The House on Mango Street* (Arte Público Press), won the Before Columbus

Foundation American Book Award. She has received a fellowship from the National Endowment for the Arts and is the author of two collections of poetry: *Bad Boys* (Mango Press) and *My Wicked Wicked Ways* (Third Woman Press, 1987).

*Cheryl Clarke* is a member of the editorial collective of *Conditions* magazine. She is a contributor to the anthologies *Lesbian Poetry*, *This Bridge Called My Back*, and *Home Girls*. She is the author of two books of poetry: *Narratives: Poems in the Tradition of Black Women* (Kitchen Table: Women of Color Press, 1982) and *Living as a Lesbian* (Firebrand Books, 1986).

*Jan Clausen* is a poet, fiction writer, and critic. She received a fiction fellowship in 1981 from the National Endowment for the Arts. Her recent books include a book of both poetry and prose, *Duration* (Hanging Loose Press, 1983), and a novel about lesbian parenting, *Sinking, Stealing* (Crossing Press, 1985). She is active in the feminist and Central America solidarity movements.

*Dennis Cooper* edited *Little Caesar Magazine* and Little Caesar Press from 1976 to 1983. From 1980 to 1983 he was director of programming at the Beyond Baroque Literary/Arts Center in Venice, California. His critical writings on literature, arts, performance, and film have appeared in *Art in America*, *Semiotext(s)*, *The Los Angeles Weekly*, *The Advocate*, among others. His most recent book is *Wrong* (Lapis Press, 1988).

*Sam Cornish* is founder, with his spouse, Florella Orowan, of the Fiction, Literature & the Arts Bookstore in Brookline, Massachusetts. He teaches at Emerson College in Boston and is the author of *Songs of Jubilee* (Unicorn Press, 1986).

*Jayne Cortez* is the author of six books of poetry, the most recent *Coagulations: New and Selected Poems* (Thunder's Mouth Press, 1984). She has received the Before Columbus Foundation Book Award (1980) and fellowships from the National Endowment for the Arts and the New York Creative Artists Public Service Program. She has served on several literature advisory panels. Her work has been published in many journals, and she has read her poetry alone and with music throughout the United States, West Africa, Europe, Latin America, and the Caribbean.

*Melvin Dixon* was a recipient, in 1984, of a fellowship from the National Endowment for the Arts. His books include *Change of Territory* (Callaloo Books, 1983) and *Ride Out the Wilderness: Geography and Identity in Afro-American Literature* (University of Illinois Press, 1987).

*Sharon Doubiago* is the author of short stories, criticism, essays, and poems. Her epic poem, *Hard Country* (1982), is available from West End Press. *Outlaw* (Landlock Press, 1987) is her most recent volume of poetry. She has won two Pushcart prizes, among others, and has edited and lectured widely.

*James A. Emanuel* has taught literature at universities in France and Poland and at the City University of New York, from which he recently retired. He is the author of several books of critical prose, including *Dark Symphony: Negro Literature in America* (Macmillan, 1968) and seven volumes of poetry, the latest of which is *Deadly James and Other Poems* (Lotus Press, 1987).

*Lynn Emanuel* is the author of *Hotel Fiesta* (University of Georgia Press, 1984), which won the Great Lakes Colleges Association New Writers' Award. She is an associate professor at the University of Pittsburgh and a member of the literature advisory panels for the Pennsylvania Council on the Arts, the National Endowment for the Arts, and the International Poetry Forum.

*Martín Espada* is a Puerto Rican poet whose work has appeared in literary magazines as well as in *Hispanics in the United States*, vol. 2, and *Editor's Choice*, vol. 2. He is the author of two books: *The Immigrant Iceboy's Bolero* (Waterfront Press, 1986) and *Trumpets from the Island of Their Eviction* (Bilingual Press, 1987). He was awarded a Massachusetts Artists fellowship in 1984 and a fellowship from the National Endowment for the Arts in 1986.

*Mari Evans* is an educator, writer, and musician. Formerly Distinguished Writer and Assistant Professor, Cornell University, she has taught at Indiana, Purdue, Northwestern, Washington, and SUNY at Albany. She is the author of numerous articles, four children's books, two musicals, and three volumes of poetry, including *I Am a Black Woman* and *Nightstar*. She edited *Black Women Writers, 1950–1980: A Critical Evaluation*.

*Edward Field* served in the air force during World War II as navigator in B-17's. His first book, *Stand Up, Friend, with Me*, won the Lamont Award. He has received a Guggenheim fellowship and also won the Shelley Award from the Poetry Society of America and the Prix de Rome from the Academy and Institute of Arts and Letters. He edited the anthology *A Geography of Poets* (Bantam Books). His *New and Selected Poems* (1987) is available from Sheep Meadow Press.

*Robert Glück* is the assistant director of the Poetry Center at San Francisco State University, where he teaches. He is a gay activist whose political activities include anti-nuclear and anti-interventionist actions. He is the author of a novel, a book of stories, a "book of alterations," and a recent collection of poems and short prose called *Reader* (Lapis Press, 1988).

*Gogisgi* (Carroll Arnett) is of Cherokee-French ancestry. He is Deer Clan, an enrolled member of the Overhill Band of the Cherokee Nation. He is a professor of English at Central Michigan University and was a recipient, in 1974, of a fellowship from the National Endowment for the Arts. An editor, he is also author of nine books of poems, the latest of which is *Rounds* (Cross Cultural Communications Press, 1982).

325

*Jessica Hagedorn* was born and raised in the Philippines. She is the author of *Dangerous Music* (1975) and *Pet Food & Tropical Apparitions* (1981), both published by Momo's Press. She has served on state and national literature panels and has been the recipient of numerous grants and awards. She has written many plays and performance pieces, one of which, "Mango Tango," was produced by Joseph Papp at the Public Theater in New York.

*Joy Harjo* is a member of the Creek Tribe. An assistant professor of English at the University of Colorado, Boulder, she serves on the board of directors for the Native American Public Broadcasting Consortium. She is poetry editor for *High Plains Literary Review*, a dramatic screenwriter, a musician, and the author of three books of poetry including *She Had Some Horses* (Thunder's Mouth Press, 1983).

*Eloise Klein Healy* is the author of three books of poetry: *Building Some Changes* (Beyond Baroque Foundation "New Book Award," 1976), *A Packet Beating Like a Heart* (Books of a Feather Press, 1980), and *Ordinary Wisdom* (Paradise Press, 1980). She has taught at colleges and universities and in the Feminist Studio Workshop at the Woman's Building in Los Angeles.

*Lance Henson* is a Cheyenne poet, former U.S. Marine, student of the martial arts, and member of the Cheyenne Dog Soldier Warrior Society. His work has been widely translated, and he is the author of nine volumes, including *Selected Poems, 1970-1983* (Greenfield Review Press, 1984).

*Calvin Hernton* is a novelist, essayist, and social scientist. He is the author of *Sex and Racism in America* (Doubleday, 1965) and *The Sexual Mountain and Black Women Writers* (Doubleday, 1987). A professor of black studies at Oberlin College, he has taught black and African literature for over fifteen years. His most recent book of poetry is *Medicine Man* (Reed, Cannon and Johnson, 1976).

*Juan Felipe Herrera* is the son of farmers. He is the recipient of two fellowships from the National Endowment for the Arts and four awards from the California Arts Council. He is the author of *Rebozos of Love* (Toltecas en Aztlán Press, 1974), *Exiles of Desire* (Arte Público Press, 1985), and *Facegames* (Dragon Cloud Press, 1987).

*Geary Hobson*, a Cherokee-Quapaw/Chickasaw, is a poet, short story writer, essayist, and editor. He served in the marines and later participated in the antiwar peace movement. He teaches at the University of New Mexico. His latest book is *Deerhunting and Other Poems* (Strawberry Press, 1988).

*Richard Hoffman* is a poet, fiction writer, and essayist. He has received a grant for poetry from the New Jersey Council of the Arts and a fellowship in prose from the Massachusetts Artists Foundation. He teaches high school English and is writing a curriculum for a course on the literature of fathers and sons.

*Linda Hogan,* a Chickasaw, is the author of several books of poetry and a collection of short fiction. Her most recent book, *Seeing Through the Sun* (University of Massachusetts Press, 1985), received an American Book Award from the Before Columbus Foundation.

*Barbara Helfgott Hyett* grew up in Atlantic City, New Jersey. She won a Massachusetts Artists Fellowship in 1984 and was a finalist for the Walt Whitman Prize and the Associated Writing Programs Award. Her book *In Evidence: Poems of the Liberation of Nazi Concentration Camps* was published by the University of Pittsburgh Press in 1986. She teaches poetry at Boston University and works as a poet-in-the schools in the Massachusetts Artists-in-Residence Program.

*Lawson Fusao Inada* is the author of *Before the War* (Morrow, 1971). He has taught at colleges and universities for twenty-five years and has conducted seminars on multicultural education throughout the United States and Europe. His work appears in numerous anthologies. He is co-owner of *Kids Matter,* a media and publishing company for children, and serves on the Commission on Racism and Bias in Education for the National Council of Teachers of English.

*Colette Inez* is a lecturer in comparative literature with Columbia University's Writers Program and has conducted poetry workshops throughout the United States. Her first book, *The Woman Who Loved Worms,* won the Great Lakes Colleges Association National Book Award in 1972. Her most recent collection is *Family Life* (Story Line Press).

*Lonny Kaneko* is a sansei poet whose recent chapbook *Coming Home from Camp* (Brooding Heron Press) reflects his family's experiences during and after their World War II internment in Minidoka, Idaho. His work appears in anthologies including *Breaking Silence* (Greenfield Review Press) and *Ayumi* (Japanese American Anthology Committee). He has received a fellowship from the National Endowment for the Arts and is coauthor, with Amy Sanbo, of two plays.

*Maurice Kenny,* a Mohawk, coedits *Contact II* with J. G. Cosciak. He is the publisher of Strawberry Press and for many years has been associated with *Akwesasne Notes* and *Studies in American Indian Literature* (Columbia University). His book *Blackrobe: Isaac Jogues* was given the National Public Radio Award for Broadcasting. In 1984 Kenny received the American Book Award for *The Mama Poems* (White Pine Press). His *Between Two Rivers: New and Selected Poems* is available from White Pine Press.

*Rudy Kikel* left his teaching position at Suffolk University in Boston in 1975 for a freelance career as poet, reviewer, and essayist. He has contributed essays to a variety of publications, including *The Advocate, Boston Gay Review,* and *Gay Community News,* and edits "Arts and Entertainment" and "Poetry" for *Bay Win-*

*dows*, a weekly gay and lesbian newspaper based in Boston. His latest book of poetry is *Lasting Relations* (Sea Horse Press, 1984).

*Kevin Killian* edits the literary magazine *Mirages* from San Francisco. His poems, stories, essays, and reviews have appeared in many avant-garde and gay publications. He is the author of *Desiree* (e.g. press, 1986).

*Irena Klepfisz* has taught literature and poetry and fiction workshops at a number of colleges and universities. She was the founder and editor (1976–81) of *Conditions* magazine. Her work has been included in several anthologies and her books of poetry include *Different Enclosures* (Onlywomen Press, 1985), *Keeper of Accounts* (Sinister Wisdom, 1983), and *Periods of Stress* (Out & Out Books, 1976).

*Etheridge Knight* has published his collected poems *The Essential Etheridge Knight*, which is available from the University of Pittsburgh Press (1986). He has been awarded fellowships by the Guggenheim Foundation and the National Endowment for the Arts. In 1985 he was given the Shelley Memorial Award by the Poetry Society of America.

*Geraldine Kudaka* is the author of *Numerous Avalanches at the Point of Intersection* (Greenfield Review Press, 1979). Her work has been published in a variety of anthologies and magazines.

*Joan Larkin* has published two collections of poetry: *Housework* (Out & Out Books, 1975) and *A Long Sound* (Granite Press, 1986). Her reviews have appeared in *Ms.*, *Sinister Wisdom*, and other journals. She has coedited two anthologies with Elly Gulkin: *Amazon Poetry* (Out & Out Books, 1975) and *Lesbian Poetry: An Anthology* (Persephone Press, 1981). She was a founding editor of Out & Out Books and has taught writing at Brooklyn College and Sarah Lawrence College.

*Meridel Le Sueur* was born at the beginning of the century to socially and politically active parents. She has lived in various communes in New York and the Midwest and has engaged in political actions from the Minneapolis truckers strike in 1934 to the Poor People's March in 1968. She was blacklisted in the forties and fifties. She is the author of many volumes of reportage, fiction, and poetry. Her most recent book of poetry is *Rites of Ancient Ripening* (Vanilla Press, 1975), and her selected work, *Ripening* (Feminist Press, 1982), was edited by Elaine Hedges.

*James Lewisohn* was a recipient in 1977 of a fellowship from the National Endowment for the Arts. He is the author of four books of poetry and essays and has edited four anthologies of prisoners' poetry. He makes donuts at a motel in Bar Harbor, Maine.

*Stephen Shu-Ning Liu*, son of a hermitic painter of waterlilies, was born in Fuling, China. For the New World Press (Beijing, 1982) he translated his English

328

poems into Chinese. The collection is called *Dream Journeys to China*. A recipient of a fellowship from the National Endowment for the Arts, he teaches English at Clark Community College in Las Vegas.

*George Ella Lyon* makes her living as a writer and teacher in Lexington, Kentucky. She has written critical essays, children's books, a novel, and a play. She is the author of a chapbook, *Mountain*, published by Andrew Mountain Press in 1983.

*J. D. McClatchy* is poetry editor of the *Yale Review* and teaches in the Creative Writing Program at Princeton. His newest collection of poetry is *Stars Principal* (Macmillan, 1986).

*Wilma Elizabeth McDaniel* was born in Stroud, Oklahoma, and raised in the area called the Creek Indian Nation. Her family were sharecroppers and in 1936 made the Dustbowl–Great Depression exodus to California. She worked on farms for many years. She began making up poems when she was four and has since written twelve books of poems, a short novel, and several books of stories. She writes a regular column for *Valley Voice*, a regional newspaper.

*Naomi Long Madgett* has been an editor and publisher of Lotus Press in Detroit since 1974. In 1984 she retired from her position as professor of English at Eastern Michigan University to devote full time to the press and her writing. She is the author of *A Student's Guide to Creative Writing* (Penway Books, 1980), and her most recent collection of poetry is *Octavia and Other Poems* (Third World Press, 1988).

*Jeff Daniel Marion* is a poet-in-residence and associate professor of English at Carson-Newman College. He is a former editor and publisher of *The Small Farm*, a literary journal. He operates Mill Springs Press and publishes poetry chapbooks and broadsides printed by letterpress. His most recent book is *Tight Lines* (Iron Mountain Press, 1981).

*Julio Marzán* was editor and chief consultant of *Faces, Mirrors, Masks: Twentieth-Century Latin American Fiction*, a thirteen-part docu-drama series produced by National Public Radio. He has reviewed books and plays for *Village Voice* and was advisor for Bilingual Children's Television's "Villa Alegre." He has received many awards and fellowships. His most recent book is *Translations Without Originals* (I. Reed Books, 1986).

*Jim Wayne Miller* is a native of the mountain country of western North Carolina. He has edited *I Have a Place*, an anthology of Appalachian writing for secondary schools, as well as Jesse Stuart's *Songs of a Mountain Plowman* and James Still's collected poems, *The Wolfpen Poems* (1986). His most recent book is *Dialogue with a Dead Man* (Green River Press, 1978).

329

*Janice Mirikitani*, a third generation Japanese American, is a poet, editor, choreographer, teacher, and community organizer. She is program director of Glide Foundation, a multicultural institution known for its social activism. She has edited three anthologies and is the author of *Shedding Silence* (Celestial Arts Press, 1976) and *Awake in the River* (Isthmus Press, 1978).

*James Masao Mitsui* is a high school teacher and a recipient of a fellowship from the National Endowment for the Arts. His books include *Journal of the Sun* (Copper Canyon Press), *Crossing the Phantom River* (Greywolf Press), and *After the Long Rain* (The Bieler Press).

*José Montoya* helped found a cultural collective called the Royal Chicano Air Force, aka Rebel Chicano Art Front. He is a painter, muralist, graphic artist, poet, and teacher. A professor in the Department of Art Education at California State University, Sacramento, he designed a training program for art teachers called Barrio Art Program. He has read and lectured widely. His book of poetry is *El Sol y los de Abajo* (Pocho-Che, 1972).

*Cherríe Moraga* is a Chicana poet, playwright, essayist, and editor who is an instructor of writing at the University of California, Berkeley. She coedited, with Gloria Anzaldua, the anthology *This Bridge Called My Back: Writings by Radical Women of Color*, which won the Before Columbus Book Award in 1986. Her most recent collection of poetry is *Loving the War Years* (South End Press, 1983). Her play, *Giving Up the Ghost*, was published by West End Press in 1987.

*Rosario Morales* was born in New York and moved to Puerto Rico at age twenty. She has studied anthropology and has done ecological and scientific research. Her work has appeared in two anthologies and in *Getting Home Alive* (Firebrand Books, 1986).

*David Mura* is a sansei—a third generation Japanese-American. His poems have appeared in numerous literary magazines and in *Breaking Silence: An Anthology of Contemporary Asian-American Poets* (Greenfield Review Press). A fellowship from the National Endowment for the Arts and the Japan–United States Friendship Commission allowed him to live in Japan for a year, and he is presently writing a book about his travels. His essay "A Male Grief: Notes on Pornography and Addiction" (Milkweed Editions, 1987) won the Milkweed Prize in creative nonfiction. His book *After We Lost Our Way* (E. P. Dutton, 1988) won the 1988 National Poetry Series Contest.

*Duane Niatum* won the American Book Award from the Before Columbus Foundation for his fourth book, *Songs for the Harvester of Dreams* (University of Washington Press, 1981). He is the editor of two anthologies from Harper and Row: *Carriers of the Dream Wheel* (1975) and *Harper's Anthology of Twentieth-Century Native American Poetry* (1987). He is a member of the Klallam Nation of Washington

State, which is a Salishan tribe of Salmon fishermen whose name means "strong people."

*Harold Norse* has taught English and creative writing in New York and at the University of California. He has published twelve books of poetry, received a fellowship from the National Endowment for the Arts, and was nominated for the National Book Award. He is the author of *Mysteries of Magritte* (Atticus, 1984).

*Ed Ochester* is the director of the Writing Program at the University of Pittsburgh. He is editor of the Pitt Poetry Series and managing editor of the Drue Heinz Literature Prize for short fiction. His latest collection of poems is *Changing the Name to Ochester* (Carnegie-Mellon University Press, 1988).

*Simon J. Ortiz*, a poet and fiction writer, is the author of *From Sand Creek, Fight Back, Fightin'* (stories) and other books, most of which refer to the heroic struggle for a continuing human community that has compassion, integrity, and dignity. As an Acoma Pueblo Indian, he insists this struggle is tied to love of land, spirituality, and the social dynamic that is enriched by one's ethnic heritage. He is currently writing *After and Before the Lightning*.

*Raymond R. Patterson* teaches at the City College of the City University of New York. His poems have appeared in literary magazines and in the *Norton Introduction to Literature* and *A Geography of Poets*. He has received a fellowship from the National Endowment for the Arts and an award from the New York Creative Artists Public Service Program. He is the author of *Elemental Blues* (Cross-Cultural Communications, 1983).

*Jean Pedrick* has taught poetry at Northeastern University School of Continuing Education and at the Boston Center for Adult Education. She is a founding member of Alice James Books and Rowan Tree Press, and the author of five books of poetry, including *Greenfellow* (New Rivers Press, 1981).

*Robert Peters* is a poet, critic, playwright, and actor who teaches Victorian literature and contemporary poetry at the University of California, Irvine. He is the author of the three-volume series *The Great American Poetry Bake-Off* (Scarecrow Press) and *The Peters Black and Blue Guides to Current Literary Journals* (Dust Books). His newest book is *Shaker Light* (Unicorn Press, 1987).

*Felice Picano* has published eleven books of poetry, fiction, plays, and screenplays. In 1978 he founded the Sea Horse Press and is cofounder and publisher of the Gay Presses of New York. He has been honored by the Poetry Society of America and with a PEN Syndicated Fiction Award.

*Minnie Bruce Pratt* was raised in a sawmill town in Alabama. From 1979 to 1983, she was a member of the editorial collective of *Feminary: A Lesbian Feminist*

331

*Journal for the South*. Her poetry has appeared in *Conditions, Sinister Wisdom,* and *New England Review/Bread Loaf Quarterly*, among others. Her book, *The Sound of One Fork*, is available from Inland Book Company.

*Eugene B. Redmond*, poet laureate of East St. Louis, Illinois, is a special Assistant Superintendent for Cultural Development in his home town. For fifteen years he served as professor of English and poet-in-residence in ethnic studies at California State University, Sacramento. He is the recipient of numerous fellowships and grants and his books include *In a Time of Rain and Desire: New Love Poems* (Black River Writers Press, 1973).

*Louis Reyes Rivera* has been the editor since 1976 of Shamal Books, a publishing outlet for African-American and Caribbean writers living in the United States. He is also a book designer, lecturer, and translator. He is a member of the Calabash Poets Workshop and the National Association of Third World Writers. His poetry has appeared in magazines and in the bilingual anthology *Herejes y Mitificadores* (Ediciones Huracan, P.R., 1980). His most recent book is *This One for You* (Shamal Books, 1983).

*Al Robles* was born in a mixed neighborhood of "blacks-chicanos-chinese-japanese-filippinos-russians-jews-appalachians & a few sea gypsies." He is a poet, writer, and oral historian who collects records, tales, stories, myths, rituals, dreams, and songs of a forgotten tribal people called "the manilatown mangos."

*Aleida Rodríguez* was born in Güines, Havana, Cuba, six years before the revolution. She has published her poetry and prose in many small magazines and has been anthologized in *Lesbian Fiction* (Persephone Press, 1981), *Fiesta in Aztlán* (Capra Press), and others. For six years she coedited and copublished *rara avia* magazine and Books of a Feather. Her prose poems, *Punto de Vista* (1987), are available from Lapis Press.

*Kate Rushin* is a feminist poet and teacher with a background in theater and independent radio. She teaches writing workshops for adults and children, and her work has been published in journals and in the anthology *This Bridge Called My Back*. She is a member of Boston Women's Community Radio and of the New Words Bookstore Collective.

*Vern Rutsala* teaches at Lewis and Clark College in Portland, Oregon. His work has appeared in numerous magazines, and he is the recipient of Guggenheim and National Endowment for the Arts fellowships. His eleventh book is *Ruined Cities* (Carnegie-Mellon University Press, 1987).

*Ron Schreiber* is one of the editors of Hanging Loose Press and magazine. In 1968 he edited *Thirty-one New American Poets* (Hill and Wang, 1968), and his most recent volumes of poetry are *Tomorrow Will Really Be Sunday* (Calamus Books, 1984) and *John* (Hanging Loose/Calamus Books, 1988).

332

*Susan Sherman* is a poet, essayist, and editor of *Ikon*, a feminist political/ cultural journal. She has published three collections of poetry and a translation of a Cuban play, *Shango de Ima* (Doubleday). Her work has been anthologized in *The East Side Scene, American Poetry, 1960–1965* (Doubleday), and *Lesbian Poetry* (Persephone Press), and her book *With Anger/With Love, Selections: Poems and Prose, 1963–1972* was published by Mulch Press.

*Beverlyjean Smith* is a dancer and former poetry editor of *Sojourner*. She was a poet-in-residence for Urban Arts (City of Boston) and a recipient of a Brookline Artists fellowship. She has taught English for seventeen years, the last eleven of which have been at Brookline High School.

*Carmen Tafolla* is a scholar, screenplay writer, educational consultant, and poet. She has published a children's collection, a book of commentary on racism, sexism, and Chicana women, and three books of poetry, the latest of which, *Sonnets to Human Beings* (Bilingual Review/Press, 1988), won first place in the poetry division of the University of California's Irvine National Chicano Literary Competition.

*David Trinidad* was editor and publisher of Sherwood Press from 1981 to 1984. His work has appeared in numerous publications and in *Coming Attractions: An Anthology of American Poets in Their Twenties* (Little Caesar Press, 1980). He is the author of *November* (Hanuman Books, 1986).

*Quincy Troupe* is a professor of American and Third World literature at the College of Staten Island (CUNY) and also teaches in Columbia University's Graduate Writing Program. He is an editor of two anthologies, coeditor of the literary journal *River Styx*, biographer, essayist, and screenwriter. His book *Snake-Back Solos* won the 1980 American Book Award for Poetry, and his most recent book is *Skulls Along the River* (I. Reed Books, 1984).

*Kitty Tsui* was born in the Year of the Dragon in the City of Nine Dragons, Kowloon, Hong Kong. She is a writer, artist, actor, and competitive bodybuilder. Her work has appeared in *Breaking Silence: An Anthology of Contemporary Asian American Poets* (Greenfield Review Press, 1983) and *Out from Under: Sober Dykes and Our Friends* (Spinsters, Ink, 1983). Her collection of poetry is *The Words of a Woman Who Breathes Fire* (Spinsters, Ink, 1983).

*Alma Luz Villanueva* is of Mexican-German descent. She is a poet and novelist whose work has appeared in various magazines and anthologies such as *Women Poets of the World* (Macmillan) and *Hispanics in the United States*. Her most recent book of poetry is *Life Span* (Place of Herons Press, 1985).

*Tino Villanueva* has worked as a migrant worker, an assembly line worker, and an army clerk in the Panama Canal Zone. He is a professor in the Spanish department at Wellesley College and the publisher and editor of the Boston-based *Imagine: International Poetry Journal* and Imagine Publishers. He is the author of

**333**

*Hay Otra Voz* (Edit Mensaje, 1979) and his most recent book of poetry is *Shaking Off the Dark* (Arte Público Press, 1984).

*Roberta Hill Whiteman* is a Wisconsin Oneida who teaches English at the University of Wisconsin–Eau Claire. She has taught at Sinte Gleska College in Rosebud, South Dakota, and participated in Poet-in-the-Schools in the Midwest and Southwest. She is a recipient of a fellowship from the National Endowment for the Arts, and her first collection, *Star Quilt* (Holy Cow Press, 1984), won the Council of Wisconsin Writers' Award in Poetry.

*Jonathan Williams* is poet, essayist, photographer, publisher of the Jargon Society since 1951, and occasional hiker of long distances. His recent books include *The Magpie's Bagpipe* (essays) from North Point Press (1982), *Blues & Roots/Rue & Bluets* (Appalachian poems) from Duke University Press (1985), *In the Azure over the Squalor* (quote book) from Gnomon Press, and *Get Hot or Get Out: A Selection of Poems, 1957–1981* from Scarecrow (1982).

*Nellie Wong* was born in the Year of the Dog and is the author of two books of poetry, *Dreams in Harrison Railroad Park* (Kelsey Street Press, 1977) and *The Death of Long Steam Lady* (West End Press). She works as an administrative assistant at the University of California, San Francisco, and is active in the clericals' union, AFSCME 3218, the Freedom Socialist Party, and Radical Women. She speaks, writes, organizes, and runs a sticker art company called Piggy Gee Productions.

*Ray A. Young Bear* is a lifetime resident of the Mesquakie (Red Earth) Tribal Settlement in central Iowa. His poems have appeared in numerous anthologies including *Harper's Anthology of Twentieth-Century Native American Poetry* and *Carrying the Darkness* (Avon Books). His two books from Harper and Row are: *Winter of the Salamander* and *Stories from the Woodland Region*. His most recent volume is *Invisible Musician* (Holy Cow Press, 1988).

*Yvonne* is a poet, filmmaker, fiction writer, and former poetry editor of *Ms.* magazine (1973–86). She has published two volumes of *The Iwilla Trilogy*: *Iwilla/Soil* and *Iwilla/Scourge* (Chameleon Productions, 1985, 1986), and the last volume was published in 1988. She has received two fellowships from the National Endowment for the Arts, a Mary Roberts Rinehart fellowship, and a grant from the New York Creative Artists Public Service Program.

# The Editors

Marie Harris is the author of two collections of poetry: *Raw Honey* (Alice James Books, 1975) and *Interstate* (Slow Loris Press, 1980). She is a freelance writer, editor, and partner, with her husband, Charter Weeks, in Isinglass Studio, an industrial advertising agency.

Kathleen Aguero is the author of two collections of poetry: *Thirsty Day* (Alice James Books, 1977) and *The Real Weather* (Hanging Loose Press, 1987). A recipient of a Massachusetts Artists Fellowship in poetry, she has also published reviews. She has taught writing and worked in the Poets-in-Residence Program for many years.

Marie Harris and Kathleen Aguero are coeditors of the collection of essays *A Gift of Tongues: Critical Challenges in Contemporary American Poetry* (University of Georgia Press, 1987).